About the Author

Dr Pat Ellis, a Barbadian, is a consultant in development, community development and gender issues. A committed feminist and trainer, she has long been in the forefront of research, education and policy advice in relation to women, and more recently has researched the problems faced by Caribbean men and issues of gender equity and gender equality. From 1986 to 1996 she was Programme Consultant for the Women and Development Unit (WAND) at the University of the West Indies. She runs an annual colloquium on particular Caribbean themes – topics so far have included The Challenge of Ageing; Organizational Change; and Lonely at the Top (the latter directly specifically at top Caribbean women executives in the public and private sectors).

In addition to numerous reports and policy documents, she has written a set of *How To Do It* booklets on effective community development. Her books include *Women of the Caribbean* (Zed Books, 1986).

Women, Gender and Development in the Caribbean

REFLECTIONS AND PROJECTIONS

PATRICIA ELLIS

Zed Books
LONDON & NEW YORK

Ian Randle Publishers
KINGSTON, JAMAICA

Women, Gender and Development in the Caribbean was first published by
Zed Books Ltd, 7 Cynthia Street, London N1 9JF, UK and
Room 400, 175 Fifth Avenue, New York, NY 10010, USA.

www.zedbooks.demon.co.uk

First published in Jamaica, 2003 by
Ian Randle Publishers, 11 Cunningham Avenue,
P.O. Box 686, Kingston 6
www.ianrandlepublishers.com

Cover designed by Andrew Corbett
Typeset in 10½/13 pt Goudy by Long House, Cumbria, UK
Printed and bound in the United Kingdom
by Biddles Ltd, Guildford and King's Lynn

Distributed in the USA exclusively by Palgrave, a division of
St Martin's Press, LLC,175 Fifth Avenue, New York, NY 10010

A catalogue record for this book is available from the British Library
Library of Congress Cataloging-in-Publication Data is available
A catalogue record for this book is available from the National Library of Jamaica

ISBN   Hb 1 85649 932 4 (Zed Books)
        Pb 1 85649 933 2 (Zed Books)
        Pb 976-637-127-X (Ian Randle)

Contents

Tables & Figures

Abbreviations

ACCA	Association of Canadian Community Colleges
AWOJ	Association of Women's Organizations in Jamaica
BIDC	Barbados Investment and Development Corporation
BOWAND	Belize Organization for Women and Development
BPWC	Business and Professional Women's Club
BWU	Barbados Workers' Union
CAEP	Caribbean Agriculture Extension Project
CAFRA	Caribbean Association of Feminist Research and Action
CANSAVE	Canadian Save the Children
CAPE	Caribbean Advanced Proficiency Examination
CARDATS	Caribbean Agriculture and Rural Development Advisory and Training Services
CATVET	Caribbean Association of Technical and Vocational Education and Training
CARDI	Caribbean Agriculture Research and Development Institute
CARICOM	Caribbean Community
CARIPEDA	Caribbean Peoples Development Agency
CARIWA	Caribbean Women's Association
CAWE	Caribbean Association of Women Entrepreneurs
CBOs	Community-based organizations
CCA	Caribbean Conservation Association
CCC	Caribbean Conference of Churches
CDB	Caribbean Development Bank
CEDAW	Convention on the Elimination of All Forms of Discrimination Against Women
CEHI	Caribbean Environmental Health Institute
CIDA	Canadian International Development Agency

CORE	Communities Organizing for Self Reliance
CPDC	Caribbean Policy Development Centre
CSME	CARICOM Single Market and Economy
CXC	Caribbean Examinations Council
DAWN	Development Alternatives with Women for a New Era
DNCW	Dominica National Council of Women
EAW	Electrical Association of Women
ECCB	Eastern Caribbean Development Bank
ECLAC	Economic Commission For Latin America and the Caribbean
EFA	Education For All
FAO	Food and Agriculture Organization
GEM	Gender Empowerment Measure
IICA	Inter American Institute for Cooperation on Agriculture
IFAD	International Fund for Agricultural Development
ILO	International Labour Organization
IMF	International Monetary Fund
ISER	Institute of Social and Economic Research
JTURDC	Joint Trade Unions' Research and Development Centre
MAVAW	Men against Violence Against Women
MESA	Men's Education and Support Association
NAFTA	North American Free Trade Agreement
NDF	National Development Foundation
NGO	Non-governmental organization
NOW	National Organization of Women
OECS	Organization of Eastern Caribbean States
PAREDOS	Parent Education for Development in Barbados
PIOJ	Planning Institute of Jamaica
RNM	Regional Negotiating Machinery
SMEs	Small and medium-size enterprises
SPAT	Small Projects Assistance Team
UG	University of Guyana
UNDP	United Nations Development Programme
UNIFEM	United Nations Development Fund for Women
UWI	University of the West Indies
WAND	Women and Development Unit
WICP	Women in the Caribbean Project
WID	Women in Development
WTO	World Trade Organization
YWCA	Young Women's Christian Association

CHAPTER 1

Women in the English-speaking Caribbean: an Overview

The English-speaking Caribbean, also known as the Commonwealth Caribbean, is comprised of a number of islands and two mainland countries, Belize in Central America and Guyana in South America. The islands vary in size and are spread in an arc from the southern tip of Florida in the north to the northern shores of Venezuela in the south. They include Anguilla, Antigua and Barbuda, the Bahamas, Barbados, Belize, the British Virgin Islands, the Cayman Islands, Dominica, Grenada, Carriacou and Petit Martinique, Guyana, Jamaica, Montserrat, St Kitts–Nevis, St Lucia, St Vincent and the Grenadines, Trinidad and Tobago, and the Turks and Caicos Islands. The islands fall into several geographical groupings. Jamaica in the north is part of the group of larger islands referred to as the Greater Antilles. The smaller islands are referred to as the Lesser Antilles and these are divided into the Leeward Islands in the north and the Windward Islands in the south. The Leeward and Windward Islands are also known as the Eastern Caribbean states. Several of these countries – including the Bahamas, Grenada, Carriacou and Petit Martinique, and St Vincent and the Grenadines – are multi-island states.

Population

According to the last census (1990–1), the total population of the countries of the Commonwealth Caribbean was 5.4 million and 50.8 per cent were women. The census also revealed that in several countries

Table 1.1 Population of Caribbean countries (1990-1 census)

Country	Population (000s)	% Male	% Female
Antigua/Barbuda	59,355	48.2	51.8
Bahamas	255,049	49.2	50.8
Barbados	260,491	47.5	52.5
Belize	210,000	51	49
British Virgin Islands	16,115	51.3	48.7
Dominica	69,463	49.7	50.3
Grenada	85,123	49.2	50.8
Guyana	701,704	49.2	50.8
Jamaica	2,366,067	48.9	51.1
Montserrat	10,639	49.7	50.3
St Kitts—Nevis	40,618	49.1	50.9
St Lucia	133,308	48.5	51.5
St Vincent & the Grenadines	106,499	49.9	50.1
Trinidad & Tobago	1,125,128	50	50

Source: Mondesire and Dunn (1997: 10).

a significant percentage of the population was young people under the age of 35. At the same time in a few of these countries, for example in Barbados, there has been a significant increase in the number of persons over 60. Given that in most countries the life expectancy rate is higher for women than it is for men, governments will face the challenge of developing policies to address the needs of older men and women, and of providing services and programmes to meet the particular needs of older women.

Traditionally, migration of people from the region has been responsible for and contributed to shifts in the population. According to a World Bank Report (1993), migration rates in the Caribbean are the highest in the world. Moreover, in some countries migration rates among women are higher than those among men, and over the years thousands of women from all strata of society have migrated to the UK and North America in search of better income-earning opportunities. At the same time many women from the smaller islands have migrated to larger, more developed countries like Jamaica, Trinidad and Barbados. While these migrant women are sometimes forced to accept low-paid jobs in their new countries, many have been able to send back remittances and other items to improve the economic situation of their families.

However, because many of these migrant women were single parents and heads of households their absence has had an effect on the demographic profile in several countries. The practice of leaving children either with mothers or other relatives and guardians resulted in the creation of families that were comprised of several young children and an older female – grandmothers, aunts or cousins. In recent years, several women and men who migrated during the 1950s and 1960s have been returning to the region. Many of the returning nationals are retirees and their presence is also beginning to change the demographic picture in several countries of the region.

Political structure

All of the countries in the English-speaking Caribbean are former colonies of Great Britain and while the majority gained independence in the 1960s and 1970s, the British Virgin Islands, the Cayman Islands, Montserrat, and the Turks and Caicos Islands are still British Overseas Territories. The independent countries have adopted the Westminster model of government with a two-party system in which parliament is comprised of a lower and upper chamber. An elected government and opposition sit in the lower house and an appointed senate in the upper house. Six of the independent countries – Antigua, Belize, Dominica, Guyana, Jamaica, St Lucia, and Trinidad and Tobago – have a decentralized, local government structure that in some cases is comprised of elected bodies and in others of nominated members. While there has been a small increase in the number of women in parliaments, in all countries men still dominate the highest positions of political power.

Although each of the countries is a separate entity, they are linked to and interact with each other on many levels and in many different ways through a number of regional institutions and organizations. The main regional and sub-regional political groupings are the Caribbean Community (CARICOM) with a secretariat in Guyana, and the Organization of Eastern Caribbean States (OECS) with a secretariat in St Lucia. These institutions provide fora in which heads of government and their ministers meet to discuss and make decisions about policies, and to agree on strategies to address matters of mutual concern like security, international relations, trade agreements, education and women's affairs. More recently countries of the region became members of the Association of Latin American and Caribbean States. Other regional governmental institutions include the Caribbean Development Bank (CDB), the Eastern Caribbean Central Bank (ECCB) and the Caribbean Environmental Health Institute (CEHI).

There are also a number of regional educational institutions that cater to the educational and professional needs of the population. Among these is the University of the West Indies (UWI), with three main campuses at Mona in Jamaica, St Augustine in Trinidad and Cave Hill in Barbados, and with a physical presence in all of the non-campus territories through its School of Continuing Studies. Through its Distance Education Programmes UWI also provides opportunities for students in the non-campus countries to access and participate in its various academic and non-academic programmes. Another regional educational institution is the Caribbean Examinations Council (CXC), the body with responsibility for administering the secondary school leaving examinations.

A number of regional and national non-governmental organizations (NGOs) and community-based organizations (CBOs) also play important roles in facilitating personal, national and regional development. They operate in all sectors of the society and cover the political, economic, social and cultural dimensions of life in the region. Some regional organizations are autonomous but others are umbrella organizations whose membership is made up of representatives of similar organizations that exist at the national level in several different countries. Among these are the Caribbean Policy Development Centre (CPDC), the Caribbean Association of Economists, the Caribbean Council of Churches (CCC), the Caribbean Conservation Association (CCA), the Caribbean Association of Feminist Research and Action (CAFRA) and the Caribbean Women's Association (CARIWA).

The economies

Caribbean countries have small open economies and, apart from Trinidad, Jamaica and Guyana, in which mineral resources provide the base for some industries, most islands are dependent on agriculture, tourism and remittances from abroad. The disadvantages faced by their small economies in competing on the world market, their reliance on a small number of cash crops for export, and the inability of the agricultural sector to feed their populations leaves these countries vulnerable to global trends and to the changes in international trading agreements. For example, in the late 1980s poor economic returns and dependency on development aid led several countries to resort to borrowing from the World Bank and the International Monetary Fund (IMF) and to implement structural adjustment programmes. As a result, currencies were devalued at the same time that the cost of imported goods escalated and greater emphasis was placed on export-oriented production and on the creation of export-processing zones. Moreover, these free trade zones benefited from incentives – often, it is said, at the expense of female workers.

> Government bends over backward for the companies in the free trade zones. They don't pay any attention to what happens to the workers, they say that what happens in here is the owners' business. The Free Zone is a state unto itself.

Structural adjustment programmes also required governments to reduce spending on the public services and on education, health care and social welfare. While these programmes were supposed to stimulate economic growth, there is evidence that, rather than doing so, they create hardships for workers, women, the poor and other vulnerable groups in the society. Their negative impact was especially felt by women, many of whom were employed in the social service sector and lost their jobs, and all of whom were expected to take full responsibility for the care of children, the elderly and the sick and to 'take up the slack' left by the reduction in social and welfare services.

In 1997 the United Nations Development Fund for Women (UNIFEM) undertook an investigation into the gender implications of trade policies in the Caribbean. The research was carried out in Barbados, Jamaica and St Lucia, and examined the impact of the North American Free Trade Agreement (NAFTA) on their economies, and specifically on those sectors in which large numbers of women were employed. The results showed the negative effect of the Agreement on the economies of St Lucia and Jamaica and on women employed in the manufacturing sector, especially in the garment and electronic assembly industries; and that, within two years of its signing, Jamaica's exports of garments to the USA had declined by 12 per cent, while Mexico's grew by 40 per cent (UNIFEM 1999: 7).

The creation of the European Union, the subsequent creation of trade barriers and the removal of preferential treatment for bananas exported to the UK contributed to a 20 per cent decline between 1991 and 1992 in banana exports. This has had a serious negative effect not only on the economies of the Windward Islands, but on the women and men employed in the banana industry and consequently on the quality of life of a significant proportion of the population in these islands. In St. Lucia between 1993 and 2000, over 3,000 farmers were adversely affected. If their family members are included, between 6,000 and 12,000 people would have felt the impact of the decline of the banana industry, and a significant number of these would have been women (Cargil 1998). A study conducted with women in 200 households in rural communities in the Windward Islands also revealed that the women felt that their living conditions had worsened because of the fall in banana prices (CAFRA 1998).

The standard of living had dropped drastically since bananas failed.

Banana flopping had a bad effect on families, the men had to leave home and migrate to look for work, women with children lost their small income.

Globalization, the creation of new trading blocs, trade liberalization, new trade agreements like NAFTA, new international economic agreements and the policies set by organizations like the World Trade Organization (WTO) have brought into sharp focus the vulnerability of the small economies of Caribbean countries and the challenges that they face in competing in a boundary-less global marketplace. Caribbean countries are therefore not only having to rethink their economic policies and to diversify the base of their economies, but are creating mechanisms and adopting strategies to enable them to compete in the global marketplace and to participate more effectively in external trade negotiations. Among these are the CARICOM Single Market and Economy (CSME) and the Regional Negotiating Machinery (RNM), intended to provide strategic guidance by identifying the interests of member countries, to build consensus among member states on extra-regional trade relations, and to provide technical assistance and training to improve and increase negotiation skills, thus enhancing the capacity of members states to negotiate more effectively and successfully in the global marketplace.

Agriculture

Agricultural activity is part of the legacy of the plantation system, and although over the years there has been a steady decline in agriculture it is still one of the main contributors to the economy in most Caribbean countries. While in some countries monocrop agriculture is a viable activity, dependence on one crop for export and generation of foreign exchange leaves several countries vulnerable to international market forces, as has been the case in the Windward Islands because of the removal of preferential agreements. As a result, several governments have implemented agricultural diversification programmes in order to revitalize and expand the agriculture sector and more attention is now being given to the production of food crops.

Although in some countries a few large plantations still exist, small-scale agriculture is common and large numbers of farmers live in rural communities and work on one or more plots of between four to five acres. In addition, large numbers of women are employed in the agriculture sector and are engaged in the production and marketing of agricultural produce. Over the last two decades, as a result of the emphasis placed on women's contribution to development, governments have begun to pay more attention to the gender division of labour in the agricultural sector, to the women's role in and contribution to agriculture, and to the needs of female agricultural workers.

Manufacturing and industry

During the last three decades, in an attempt to expand their economies and to shift from total reliance on monocrop agriculture to export-led growth based on manufacturing and industry, several Caribbean countries have adopted a strategy of industrialization. They have provided financial incentives and facilities for foreign investors and the promise of cheap, mainly female, labour. Initially, the garment and electronics industries based on assembly line manufacturing were introduced in several countries; within the last decade, however, the informatics and financial services industries have come into prominence, employing thousands of women at very low wages.

Tourism

Tourism is gradually replacing agriculture as the driving force of economic growth and development in several Caribbean countries and governments are investing a significant amount of financial and human resources in developing and expanding the industry. Moreover, steps are being taken to diversify by increasing cruise-ship, eco-, heritage and cultural tourism, and by promoting niche and up-market tourism. Consequently, tourism now contributes a significant amount to the revenue of several countries and in some – Antigua, the Bahamas and Barbados, for example – it is becoming the main foreign exchange earner. However, several activities linked to tourism have led to social problems like drugs, male and female prostitution and the spread of HIV/AIDS and other sexually transmitted diseases.

Women are employed at all levels of the tourist industry and, as in other service industries, mainly in the lower echelons. One offshoot of tourism has been the development of sex tourism and the increase in the number of sex workers. Between 1997 and 1998 CAFRA implemented a Research Project on Tourism and the Sex Trade in the Caribbean. The study, carried out in Barbados, Belize, Guyana and Jamaica, sought to examine the links and relationship between tourism and prostitution. The research findings showed that because of lack of employment and economic opportunities women often migrated to other countries in the hope of finding work, but because they had few marketable skills and few options, they were vulnerable and open to exploitation and often had to resort to prostitution.

Small enterprise development

According to Moore and Whitehall (2000) the micro and small business sector is an integral part of small open economies because small businesses absorb surplus labour and create employment and opportunities for entrepreneurs to exploit niche markets and to provide new products and services.

Following the declaration of 1988 as the Year of Small Business, there has been an increase in the number and type of small and medium-sized businesses in all Caribbean countries and more attention has been paid to promoting and providing support to facilitate their growth and development. While there is no precise definition of micro, small or medium enterprises, and no clearly stated policies or formal institutional arrangements to coordinate or evaluate them, they are recognized as a distinct economic sector that is creating and increasing employment opportunities. It accounts for 45 per cent of jobs created, for over 70 per cent of export agriculture crops and for a high proportion of domestic food crops. Moreover, small or medium-sized businesses now account for between 70 and 80 per cent of all enterprises in the region. The majority of these enterprises are part of

Table 1.2 Allocation of large and small businesses by sector (Barbados)

Category	Small businesses	Large businesses	Total	% Small businesses
Agriculture	18,000	126	1,826	99
Manufacturing	42	230	272	15
Wholesale/Retail	1,354	91	1,445	94
Construction	25	10	35	71
Services	3,364	211	3,575	94
Total	22,785	668	23,453	97

Source: Barbados Institute of Management and Productivity.

the informal sector and nearly half of them are wholesale and retail businesses (ILO POS 2000).

Small businesses are defined as those having less than 20 employees. They can be found in all major sectors of the economy and, as Table 1.2 shows, in Barbados it is estimated that firms employing less than 20 persons conduct 97 per cent of business activity (*ibid.*)

In several countries significant numbers of women own businesses that they have started from their own savings, often accumulated through informal schemes ('Su Su', 'box' or 'meeting turn')[1] or with money borrowed from relatives. Women own from about a third to well over a half of all businesses in the region. For example, in Dominica women own about half of the commercial enterprises, and in Barbados in 1993, of the 890 new businesses registered, just under one third (30.7 per cent) were owned by women (Barbados Report to the UN 1995).

Lack of access to finance often limits the growth and development of small businesses and in many cases entrepreneurs in this sector experience difficulty in accessing start-up funds from formal financial institutions in the banking sector. As a result, in several countries a number of financial institutions geared to providing finance to small and micro businesses have emerged. Among these have been national development foundations, small business units, enterprise funds and credit unions. Because the collateral required and the interest rates charged by these institutions are significantly lower than those of commercial banks, entrepreneurs now have greater access to credit. In addition, many of them also provide training in financial management to their clients. Significant numbers of women have been able to access start-up funds from these organizations and have acquired skills that have enabled them to develop and operate successful businesses.

Education

In the Caribbean, education has always been highly regarded not only as necessary for obtaining employment and social mobility, but also for promoting productivity, economic growth and national development, and enhancing the quality of life of the population. Many Caribbean governments therefore allocate a significant proportion of their national budgets to education. Over the last decade, however, growing concern about the increase of functional illiteracy and about the failure of the formal education system to equip students for the world of work and for functioning effectively in the new century has caused many governments to reform their education systems. The aim is to make education more relevant and more responsive to the needs of the population and of the country. Examples of these initiatives can be found in several policy documents, in the subsequent reforms in curricula and in the emphasis on technology at all levels of the system. Among the policy documents are the White Paper on Education Reform (Barbados, 1995), the State Paper on Education Policy (Guyana,

Table 1.3 Regional enrolment ratios (1990)

Level	% Male	% Female
Pre-Primary	38.5	39.4
Primary	84.7	82.2
Secondary	41	46.9
Tertiary	3.7	4.6

Source: Mondesire and Dunn (1997: 19).

1995), Learning and Growing: the Long-Term Education Plan (St Kitts–Nevis, 1998–2011) and the OECS Education Reform Strategy (1991). All of these and other similar documents set out plans and strategies for reforming education systems in Caribbean countries.

In all countries there is equal access and opportunity for males and females to pursue education up to university level. Universal primary education is the norm in all countries and universal secondary the norm in most. Education is free from nursery to university and at the tertiary level there is the University of the West Indies. In addition there are technical and vocational institutes and polytechnics, as well as community and professional colleges in most countries.

Figures for 1990 show that only at the primary level are there more males than females enrolled in education institutions, and in the last few years there has been an increase in the number of females enrolled at all levels of the education system. This is especially so at the tertiary level. In Trinidad and Tobago, for example, female enrolment in 2000 was 49 per cent at the primary level, 50 per cent at secondary level and 54 per cent at university – up from 49 per cent in the 1980s (Republic of Trinidad and Tobago 2000).

Except in St Kitts–Nevis, children between the ages of 10 and 11+ must sit and pass an examination in order to qualify for free secondary education. Throughout the region there are various types of secondary school, including grammar, comprehensive, and technical schools operated by government and private fee-paying schools. At the end of five years students sit a Secondary Schools Examination offered by the CXC; after a further two years they may sit the recently offered Caribbean Advanced Proficiency Examination (CAPE), or the long-standing Advanced Level Examination offered by Cambridge University.

There appears to be a wide gap between male and female participation at the upper levels of the secondary and at the tertiary levels in several countries, however, and significant numbers of males are dropping out of secondary school and failing to complete their formal education and to obtain certificates. As a result, over the last decade participation, performance and achievement of males have become matters of concern for many.

Since 1990 Chief Education Officers in the region have expressed grave concern about the poor performance of boys at all levels of the education system and since then the debate has continued, as has the search for factors that contribute to this phenomenon. Records of educational institutions show that more girls than boys are enrolled in nursery school and that at the primary school level girls attend more frequently than boys and therefore have more opportunities to learn. Moreover, observations in some classrooms in Jamaica showed that in most cases boys showed less interest in academic work; they were less eager to answer questions and to undertake and complete academic tasks (Evans 1999).

Over the last few years examination results at the primary, secondary and tertiary levels also show that in terms of educational achievement females are outperforming males. In several countries girls top the Eleven Plus Examination, the gateway to secondary education, and at the secondary level (the CXC examinations) over the last few years more girls have entered and they have achieved higher grades than boys.

In Jamaica in 1997 63.9 per cent of females and 36.1 per cent of males were entered for the General Proficiency Level of the CXC examinations. The pass rate in the academic subjects was 45.0 per cent for females and 36.4 per cent for boys, but in the vocational subjects it was 51.1 per cent for boys and 50.2 per cent for girls. Overall, boys had better results in mathematics and integrated science and girls in the humanities and social sciences. The results also showed that boys in coeducational schools obtained better results than those in single-sex schools (Bailey 2000: 53).

At the tertiary level there are more women than men in the graduating classes on the various campuses of the UWI. In 1997 at Jamaica's Mona campus, males (5.7 per cent) obtained a higher pass rate with first-class honours than did females (4.7 per cent) On the St Augustine campus in Trinidad, however, women outperformed men in every discipline except medicine and engineering at the undergraduate level. In 2000, 75 per cent of the graduates on Mona campus were women, and a woman was placed first in the medical examinations and received the medal for the beat student on all three campuses. In 2001, 83 per cent of the 128 graduates in law were women and 12 of these, as opposed to three males, were on the principal's honour roll. At the graduation ceremony in 2000 the Chancellor of the UWI expressed concern about the small number of males in the university and about the small number of male graduates.

The performance and achievement of males has become an issue of great concern throughout the region and in some countries – in Barbados, for example – there is an ongoing debate about the effects of coeducation, the feminization of the teaching service and the absence of males in the classroom on the poor performance of males. At the same time others draw attention to the fact that higher educational performance and achievement by females is not a new phenomenon. They cite evidence from the 1946 results of the Cambridge examinations to show that girls obtained 64 per cent of the passes compared to 50 per cent obtained by boys in single-sex schools (Blackman 2000).

Recent research on gender in education conducted in Jamaica has shown that although fewer males are gaining certification in secondary level and in university examinations, those males are still doing well in scientific and technical areas (Bailey 2000), and that many factors contribute to gender differences in performance – including the school environment, teacher–student interaction that appears to be biased in favour of girls, and teaching methods that appear to alienate boys (Evans 1999). The Evans study of gender differences in academic achievement, participation and opportunity to learn, carried out in various types of secondary schools, was commissioned by the Ministry of Education and Culture and was an attempt to find out why boys were achieving less than girls and how the school was contributing to this phenomenon. One outstanding finding of this study was that 'boys actively and continuously constructed a definition of themselves as irresponsible, unreliable, and uninterested in academic work' (*ibid.*: 53) In addition, some boys are viewing education as feminine: the more females succeed in this area, the more it will be regarded by these boys as feminine and sissy.

In response to this concern about male participation, performance and achievement in education, in some schools special programmes are being implemented to motivate and support male students. One such programme has recently been implemented in an all-boys primary school in Barbados. Within this programme a number of men who have succeeded against the odds serve as mentors. They interact with the boys and organize activities designed to inculcate sound values and desirable attitudes, to enhance their understanding of the role and responsibilities of males in the society, and to shape their future. According to the (female) principal, the programme has created a healthy and competitive environment in the school, and it has resulted in a change in the boy's deportment, and in their attitudes to work and to each other.

In spite of the higher achievement of females in Caribbean societies where academic qualifications are the prerequisite for obtaining employment, research has shown that, in spite of lower levels of educational achievement, fewer men are unemployed than women, that unqualified males are more likely to find employment than qualified females, and that women tend to be more qualified than men holding similar positions (Planning Institute of Jamaica [PIOJ] 1997).

In spite of a significant amount of work to break down gender stereotypes in curricula and text books, to expose teachers to gender concepts and to increase their gender sensitivity, in many schools sex segregation of curricula, traditional notions of male and female subjects, and teacher bias and expectations of male and female students are still apparent, and are reflected in students' choice of subject at secondary and tertiary level. For example, males continue to predominate in the science, craft and technical subjects, and females in the arts, humanities, hospitality and food, and commerce. This of course has implications for occupational opportunities and accounts in part for the clustering of large numbers of 'female occupations' at the lower levels of the labour force in the service sector.

While there are more females participating in the formal education system than there are males, and in spite of recent reforms to the curriculum, and of a number of females pursuing studies in traditional male subjects, there is still a significant amount of gender bias: on the whole, students are still inclined to pursue studies in traditional male and female subject areas. In addition, in spite of greater participation and higher levels of performance and achievement in education, women are still being discriminated against in the workplace.

NOTE

1 These are informal saving schemes in which a group of individuals agree to pool a certain sum of money on a weekly, fortnightly or monthly basis. The individual selected to be the 'banker' collects the money from each participant and gives it to the one whose 'turn' it is to receive the total amount. In some cases, the banker receives a percentage of the total from each individual as they receive their 'hand'.

CHAPTER 2

Women at Home and at Work

There is an existing and lingering perception and belief that Caribbean women are strong, powerful, capable and able to take care of themselves and their families. This belief is born out of the history of women's ability to meet the challenges of survival during slavery, colonialism and in the era of independence; their upkeep of and commitment to the development and progress of their families; and their valuable contributions to national and regional development. There is also the belief among some that there is equality among the sexes, and that gender equality has been achieved in some countries. One of the reasons for this is probably the high rating given to some countries in the Gender Development Index and the Gender Empowerment Index (UNDP 2000b).

While for some women these perceptions and beliefs may be true, they certainly do not reflect the reality of all or even of the majority of women in the region. Ethnicity, class, age, social and marital status, and level of education are important factors that determine the status, position and condition of individual women and of particular groups of women. The belief that Caribbean societies are predominately matrifocal also obscures the fact that in reality they are patriarchal and male-dominated. Consequently, Caribbean women are still discriminated against and hold fewer positions of power at the highest levels of political decision making than men do. This is so because, in spite of the emphasis on women's role and contributions, on the reality of their position and condition, and on empowering them, perceptions

Table 2.1 Gender Empowerment Measure (GEM), ratings of selected countries (1998)

Country	GEM rank	GEM value
Barbados	17	0.629
Bahamas	16	0.633
Antigua/Barbuda	—	—
St Kitts–Nevis	—	—
Trinidad & Tobago	22	0.583
Dominica	—	—
Grenada	—	—
Belize	40	0.493
Jamaica	—	—
St Lucia	—	—

Source: UNDP *Human Development Report* (2000).

of manhood and womanhood continue to be based on traditional beliefs and gender stereotypes that have their roots in the biological argument. Moreover, significant numbers of men as well as of women hold these perceptions and beliefs. Data from research studies conducted in Barbados and in St Vincent (Barrow 1998; Ellis 1998) revealed that perceptions of manhood and womanhood and about the appropriate roles for women and men have remained virtually unchanged over three generations.

> Men and women are built differently, they cannot be the same, from tradition men and women do different things. (Male)

> Men have more willpower, women are weaker, it has to do with strength. (Female)

> Women are soft and more understanding, they are different in terms of emotions, they are made that way. Men need to be strong to carry out their responsibilities. (Male)

> Strong aggressive women are tomboys. (Female)

> Men who cry are soft, women who are strong are playing men. (Female)

Female-headed households

Women not only account for half of the population in the region but head just over a third (34.8 per cent) of the 1.3 million households. In five countries this figure is above 40 per cent; in another five it is over 30 per cent; and in four it is under 30 per cent. Moreover, there are noticeable differences between those countries with high levels of female-headed households (40 per cent and over) and those with low levels of under 30 per cent. The differences may in part result from the ethnic composition of the population and the accompanying cultural diversity, especially in Belize, Guyana, and Trinidad and Tobago. In Belize there are large Spanish-speaking and Amerindian populations; in Guyana there are significant numbers of Amerindians and Indo-Guyanese; and in Trinidad Indo-Trinidadians outnumber other ethnic groups. Religious and other cultural values and norms based on traditional gender roles, especially in relation to family and marriage, also play a major role in these societies and may therefore be a key factor that has contributed to lower levels of female-headed households than in countries like St Kitts–Nevis, Barbados, Grenada, Antigua and St Lucia, where populations are comprised mainly of people of African descent.

In many Caribbean countries, even in households in which males are reported as household heads, women are primarily responsible for managing the money and for taking major decisions. However, recent research has shown that female-headed households are among the poorest and that these household heads are among the most vulnerable women in the society (KAIRI Consultants 1999, 2000).

Female-headed households also tend to be comprised of large families. The women who head them are usually single parents with several children, sometimes fathered by several different men, many of whom do not provide regular financial or other support for their offspring. In many female-headed households fathers are therefore either unknown, absent, indifferent or irresponsible.

I don't know my father, I didn't grow up with him.

My father didn't have time, he left most things to my mother.

My mother did everything to support us, if she wasn't strong I don't know what would have happened to us.

My mother raised us without a husband.

The women in female-headed households are therefore totally responsible for the financial and emotional support of families that may also include their mothers and younger male and female siblings. Consequently, female-headed households are more likely to be intergenerational, and in several of these three-generation families only one woman may be employed. Moreover, many women who are single parents and heads of households are often either unemployed or underemployed. For example, data from a recent family life survey carried out by UWI in Trinidad and Tobago (St Bernard 1995) revealed

Table 2.2 Percentage of households headed by women

Country	% Female-headed households
Antigua	41.5
Bahamas	35.8
Barbados	43.5
Belize	20.9
British Virgin Islands	28.7
Dominica	36.9
Grenada	42.7
Guyana	28.3
Jamaica	38.0
Montserrat	39.5
St Kitts–Nevis	43.9
St Lucia	40.4
St Vincent & the Grenadines	39.3
Trinidad & Tobago	28.1

Source: Mondesire and Dunn (1997: 12).

that 15.6 per cent of female family heads had never been employed in their lifetime. Yet many women who head families may work on a seasonal or occasional basis in factories, in the service sector or in some other low-skilled, low-paid job, and have less access to resources like land and credit.

There are a lot of women with plenty children working for little money.

I work at a factory or in the cane fields, the money can't meet my needs.

Fathers are the problem, they don't support their children, the poor mothers are left to bear the strain.

Participation in the labour force

Caribbean women have always worked, and work outside of the home is an integral part of their identity. As figures in the census of 1990 and in labour force surveys and reports show, however, their participation in the labour force and in the formal sectors of the economy is lower than that of men.

In addition they are the lowest-paid in the labour force; they experience the highest rates of unemployment; and, as workers, the majority are inadequately protected.

Nevertheless, in recent years there has been an increase in the number of women in the labour force in several countries. In Trinidad and Tobago, for example, between 1990 and 1995 the number of women in the labour force increased by 21.9 per cent as compared with 6 per cent for the number of men, and their participation rate increased from 37.8 per cent in 1990 to 44.9 per cent in 1995, a growth of 7.1 percentage points, while that of males only increased from 74.3 to 75.5 per cent, a growth of 1.2 percentage points (Republic of Trinidad and Tobago 1997). In Belize, while men outnumber women in the labour force by 3.4:1, the number of working women is growing faster than the number of working men, and in 1991 the female participation rate increased by 1.8 per cent while the male participation rate decreased by 8 per cent (Belize 1994).

Table 2.3 Labour force participation (1990)

Country	Males % of labour force	Females % of labour force
Antigua	53.9	46.1
Bahamas	53.4	46.6
Barbados	54.6	45.4
Belize	76.7	23.3
British Virgin Islands	56.6	43.4
Dominica	65.5	34.5
Grenada	62.1	37.9
Guyana	74	26
Jamaica	57.1	42.9
Montserrat	58.4	41.6
St Kitts—Nevis	55.7	44.3
St Lucia	58.9	41.1
St Vincent & the Grenadines	63.8	36.2
Trinidad & Tobago	62.2	37.8

Source: Mondesire and Dunn (1997: 41).

Table 2.4 Working population by occupational group (Barbados)

Occupation	Male	Female
Legislators & administrators	180	86
Corporate managers	2,576	1,156
Life science & health professionals	495	1,361
Teaching	1,458	2,587
Office clerks	1,475	5,607
Shop assistants & market traders	1,423	3,586
Skilled agriculture & fisheries workers	2,122	315
Sales and service	4,003	7,991
Metal, machinery & trades	3,997	64
Industrial plant operators	191	6

Source: Barbados Population and Housing Census (1990).

In spite of this, and of the fact that many more women are moving into higher-paying and higher-prestige jobs, the majority are still concentrated in 'female occupations' and are still employed in jobs that are regarded as 'women's work'. In St Vincent women represent 75 per cent of the services sector, in Grenada 46 per cent, and, as Table 2.4 shows, large numbers of women in Barbados are employed in the education and health sectors and in the sales and service sectors of the economy. This pattern is repeated in most countries in the region.

Employment

The laws in most countries state that employers should not discriminate against potential employees on the basis of their sex, but as can be seen in Table 2.5 high unemployment levels among women continue to be a common feature, and in every country unemployment of females is higher than that of males. However, because of the difficulty in collecting information about the number of persons employed in the informal sector in part-time, seasonal and occasional work, and because of the large number of women working in this sector and engaged in these types of economic activities, the number of employed women may actually be higher.

While the emergence in the 1970s and 1980s of the offshore sector and of export-processing zones did provide employment opportunities for women, it also created a greater degree of sex segregation in the labour force. In term of wages, in the public sector men and women earn similar salaries, but on the whole men earn about 17 per cent more than women do, and in the private sector women earn less than men.

In the Caribbean there is a general belief that formal education and training and the acquisition of academic qualifications and certificates increases an individual's employment opportunities and possibilities of earning higher incomes. There is also evidence that more females are making use of education and training opportunities than are males. In view of this the findings of an analysis of wage earnings in Barbados based on the Continuous Household Sample Survey in 1992 shed

Table 2.5 Percentage of unemployed population by sex

Country	Males	Females
Antigua/Barbuda	23.6	40.6
Bahamas	25.8	40.6
Barbados	33.5	52.5
Belize	32.4	75.4
British Virgin Islands	18.6	33.5
Dominica	32.2	64.7
Grenada	40.6	65.4
Guyana	28.4	75.6
Montserrat	58.1	52.5
St Kitts–Nevis	27.3	45.7
St Lucia	27.6	53.4
St Vincent & the Grenadines	33.5	64.6
Trinidad & Tobago	42.3	73.1

Source: CARICOM (1991).

interesting light on the relationship between education and training and earnings among males and females (Coppin 1996).

In several countries a greater number of working women have a university education than working men. Yet the Barbados study found that while both secondary and university education were important factors in obtaining employment, younger women's education did not necessarily enhance their wages. In 1992 in Barbados and in 1993 in Trinidad and Tobago working women earned an average of 83 cents to every dollar earned by working men, and within the private sector in Barbados males with secondary education earned more than females educated to the same level. At the same time, whereas young women's earnings grew rapidly when they first entered the labour market and diminished sharply over the years, young men's earnings grew in relation to their experience. The Coppin study also revealed that young employed females enjoyed fewer training opportunities and that a greater number of working males had received and benefited from on-the-job and institutional training than working women (*ibid.*).

The findings of this study, although limited to Barbados, raise several questions about female employment in the region. In the first place, in several countries the unemployment rate is higher among young people and among young women than it is among young men: this in spite of the increase in the numbers of young women attaining higher levels of education than their male counterparts. Second, the existence of sex-biased employment policies and recruitment practices leaves many working women at a disadvantage not only in the type of jobs that they can obtain, but also in terms of remuneration, promotion and career advancement. As Coppin pointed out, many people believe that secondary education ought to lead to white-collar employment, but in Barbados 50 per cent of unemployed females under 25 years with secondary education could not obtain these jobs and were obliged to take blue-collar jobs. At the same time it is important to question whether the education system is adequately equipping females with the skills required by the rapidly changing and volatile labour market and for occupations that can command higher wages and offer greater opportunities for career development.

The formal sectors

Within the formal sectors of Caribbean economies the majority of employed women are service workers in low-status and low-paid jobs, or in administrative, executive and clerical occupations. In recent years as women became more educated and gained more and higher-level skills, larger numbers are to be found in the commercial sectors, the financial sectors in banking and insurance, and in a variety of professional and technical fields.

The agriculture sector

While there are still no precise data on the number of female agricultural workers, it is widely known that large numbers of women are employed as seasonal and occasional workers to provide plantations and farms throughout the region with unskilled, low-paid labour. Moreover, even though many of these women have over the years developed some skill and speed in carrying out a variety of tasks, there is still a belief that they are incapable of improving the skills that they already have or of learning new ones. Consequently, few opportunities have been provided for them to be exposed to any type of training, or to be promoted to other areas of agricultural work.

The available data do show that that in several countries there are more female than male farmers and that large numbers of women are employed in the agricultural sector as farm operators, labourers, small or subsistence farmers, and as producers of cash crops for local and export markets. In Antigua 62.3 per cent of all farmers are women and over half (53.5 per cent) of the part-time, and just under a third (30.8 per cent) of the full-time farmers are women (Ellis 1993). In Jamaica 19.4 per cent of all farms are operated by women and 39 per cent of these farms are small. In Grenada there are 3,989 female farmers and in St Vincent 30 per cent of the agricultural labour force is female. In Jamaica 40 per cent of the landless farmers are women (Antrobus 1992), and in other countries many female farmers do not own land. They either farm on their partner's land, on family land or on rented land. Because they have no title to land and therefore no collateral, their ability to access credit from banks and other financial institutions is limited. Moreover, female farmers face this difficulty even within projects designed to provide credit for small farmers.

> [A]lthough the Development Bank ... states that it treats all applications equally, and approves loans on merit, there is an in-built discrimination of women's applications in that they often request smaller loans, and have less collateral acceptable to the bank.... (Quoted in ibid.: 8)

Most of the women in the agricultural sector are between the ages of 45 and 65 years. Women hoe, weed, plant and harvest agricultural produce, and are an important link in the regional food chain as producers and marketers of agricultural products. They are also involved in fisheries and forestry. However, although they play such important roles and make valuable contributions to the agricultural sector and to rural development, much of their contribution remains invisible because the food that they grow in backyard gardens and on small-holdings, the unpaid labour that they do on family land, and the produce that they sell in the market are not accurately recorded or reflected in national statistics.

While the majority of women in the sector are largely untrained and low-skilled, in recent years a growing number of women have been exposed to training at a number of tertiary institutions in the region and have pursued undergraduate and graduate training in the Faculty of Agriculture at UWI. As a result several female field technicians, agronomists, entomologists, horticulturalists, agricultural economists and agricultural planners can be found throughout the region.

In spite of this, there is still a fairly rigid sexual division of labour within the sector and women are therefore mostly engaged in subsistence farming while men are engaged in commercial farming. The majority of women still do not carry out activities that require strength, and the tasks that they undertake do not involve the use of machines and vehicles or technical and mechanical tools This has implications for the wages paid to males and females engaged in agricultural activities, and while there has been a move in all countries towards equal pay for work of equal value, in some countries women employed in certain areas of agriculture still receive lower wages than their male counterparts. In Antigua and Barbuda, for example, activities in which men are engaged, like harvesting or catching fish, attract higher wages than the post-harvesting activities like scaling, cleaning and selling in which most women are involved (Williams 1990).

Women in rural communities are more likely to be dependent on agriculture for their total income than their male counterparts. While they eat some of what they produce, more often than not they sell their produce and use the cash to provide food, clothes and shelter for their families while many men migrate to urban centres to seek more lucrative employment. The phenomenon of the male part-time farmer leaves women with the major responsibility for and to the hazards of operating and managing the farms.

In spite of this and of evidence to the contrary, because of a lingering perception that a farmer is a man, and that a woman on a farm is the 'farmer's wife', or 'just a housewife', many women who are engaged in farming are not regarded as farmers. In addition, women who work alongside their spouses or partners on the farm, or who provide labour on family farms or plots and grow vegetables in their backyards for home consumption, are hardly ever seen or registered as farmers. As a result, extension workers, the majority of whom are men, more often than not transmit technical information to males on the farm. Because of emphasis on the farm family, and lack of awareness and understanding about gender roles, relations and inequalities within the family, resources in many agricultural projects are planned without taking into consideration the different roles that males and females in the farm household play, and the different agricultural tasks that they undertake. Because of this, the needs of female farmers for technical agricultural information, for improved technologies, and for access to land, capital and credit are not being met within many of these projects. This is so even though in recent years more attempts have been made to address the needs of women in agriculture.

The credit programme did not benefit women directly, only 9 per cent of the women received loans. (Ibid.)

Marketing of agricultural products locally and regionally is dominated by women and many small farmers depend on them to market their produce. As higglers, hucksters, hawkers and market vendors they are responsible for selling agricultural produce in local and regional markets. In Dominica 70 per cent of the trade in agricultural crops other than bananas is undertaken by hucksters, a trade that is not limited to the English-speaking countries but spans the entire Caribbean. These women are well known for their role in transporting food crops, fruits and vegetables, and for returning home with dry goods and other merchandise not only for their own use but to sell. While there are no accurate statistics on the value of their contribution to the GDP, it is now recognized that this trade adds millions of dollars to economies in the region.

Profile of Ms B

I have been farming this two-acre plot in the project for five years. Prior to this I did domestic work, but I am making more money now. I feel a greater sense of independence and plan to stay in agriculture permanently. I rent the land for EC$100.00 per month. Last year I made a profit of about EC$1000.00.

I work very hard and although four of my seven children live with me they don't really help, they don't like farming. I plant vegetables and the Ministry of Agriculture provides some services, like seeds at reduced prices and some information. But mostly I rely on my own experience or I may ask other farmers. I don't know where else to go for information. Sometimes there are programmes on the radio, but I don't listen to them often or practise what they say.

I have got accustomed to using chemicals now but I do it on a hit-and-miss basis. I have never been to any training workshop or seminar run by the Ministry, they tend to invite the men.

I reap my own crops and sell them in the public market. I would like to sell some to the hotels but I have no transportation. Because of this some of my produce spoils. I have never taken a loan, I prefer not to credit, I don't like to owe anybody.

During the last two decades, there has been a growing recognition of the contribution of women to the agricultural sector, and a shared concern about the condition of women in rural communities among international agencies like the Food and Agriculture Organization (FAO) and the International Fund for Agricultural Development (IFAD), and regional agencies like CARICOM, CAFRA, the Caribbean Agriculture and Rural Development Advisory and Training Services (CARDATS), the Caribbean Agriculture Research and Development Institute (CARDI), the Agriculture Extension Project (CAEP) and the Women and Development Unit (WAND), together with Ministries of Agriculture in all countries. These bodies have funded and implemented several activities, programmes and projects aimed at improving the situation and condition of women in rural communities who work in the agricultural sector, enhancing their participation and valuing their contribution.

Several research projects have been undertaken and these have helped to expand the database on rural women and on women in agriculture. Among these was a project on The Role of Women in Small-Scale Agriculture in the Eastern Caribbean carried out in St Lucia in 1981 by UWI's Woman and Development Unit as part of the Caribbean Agricultural Extension Project, FAO studies on The Situation of Rural Women in the Caribbean, CAFRA's Women in Caribbean Agriculture project in Dominica and St Vincent in 1998, and research on The Role of Women in Fisheries in Antigua and Barbuda in 1990.

Many rural development projects have focused on women and provided them with training and other resources to improve their condition and to enhance their role in rural development. These included two projects implemented by WAND – the pilot project for the Integration of Women in Rural Development in Rose Hall, St Vincent in 1981, and the Integrated Rural Development Project in St Lucia, in collaboration with the National Research and Development Foundation (1983–6) – and the Integrated Rural Development Project funded by IFAD and implemented in Dominica in 1990.

Although significant numbers of women have benefited from agricultural and rural development projects and programmes, in many cases no specific plans or strategies were devised to facilitate their participation or to address their particular needs. Little if any consideration was given to women's multiple roles, or to understanding how and in what ways the performance of their reproductive roles would affect their productive roles and participation in project activities. Moreover, because most agricultural planners and project coordinators assume that women's productive role is secondary to her reproductive role, in designing these projects more attention was given to implementing 'home economics' activities like food preparation and preservation than to activities that would help women to acquire skills and thus enhance and strengthen their productive role.

Little if any consideration was given to women's health, nutritional status and general well-being. And even though some of these projects targeted women and attempted to provide them with resources and services, they were seldom designed to ensure that this actually happened, and that women had the same access to and control over the project's resources as male participants. These shortcomings in agricultural and rural development programmes and projects are the direct result of gender-blind policies. Evidence of this can be seen in the national agricultural policies formulated in the 1990s by the governments of several countries including Barbados and Grenada, as well as in the Plans of Action and programmes of regional agencies like CARICOM's Programme for Agricultural Development, the OECS Agricultural Diversification Plan, and the Plans of Action of the FAO and IICA. These were all silent on issues relating to women in agriculture. It is only in the last few years that serious attempts have been made to address women's issues and to integrate a gender perspective into national policies, plans and strategies for agricultural development and diversification.

Manufacturing and industry

Employment in the manufacturing and industrial sectors provides many women with an important source of income, and throughout the region thousands of women are employed in these sectors. Barbados was the first country to adopt a programme of export-led growth based on assembly-line manufacturing and by the 1970s there were more women in manufacturing than there were men The expansion of export-processing zones in the 1980s resulted in the creation of enclaves for the production of garments and electronic components to be exported mainly to the USA. In the 1990s the information service sector developed and several offshore data-processing factories were established. By 1989 two thirds of the employees in the manufacturing sector were females and 90 per cent of these were involved in assembling garments. In St Vincent 90 per cent of those employed in enclave industries are women and in Barbados the Statistical Report of Employment in Manufacturing and Service Companies for December 2000 shows that the 499 registered companies employed 13,742 persons of whom 6,326 (45 per cent) were women. Examination of the report reveals that women outnumbered men in the textile, apparel, and electronics industries and in information services (see Table 2.6).

Table 2.6 Male and female employees in selected industries in Barbados

Industry	Males	Females
Food and beverages	608	282
Textiles, apparel & leather	216	1,586
Electronic components & devices	123	835
Handicraft	34	89
Information services	102	1,264

Source: BIDC (December 2000).

The thousands of women employed in the garment and electronic industries in the Caribbean are part of a global assembly line comprised of women in Asia, Latin America and the Caribbean, all of whom are assembling different components of the same or similar products for multinational corporations. According to Kelly (1986), 90 per cent of all production workers in the four electronics companies in St Lucia were women. In her study Greene (1990) found that there were about 20,000 women working in 750 garment factories in the eastern Caribbean producing for the US market; in Barbados in 1989, 65 per cent of those employed in this sector were female (Massiah 1998). Most of these workers are young women under the age of 30, many of whom are not married. While some may be living in common-law relationships, a large number are single parents who are solely responsible for providing financial support for their families. For many, work in a factory on an industrial estate is preferable to working in agriculture or as a domestic servant.

In the latter half of the 1980s and in the early 1990s a number of research studies produced data on women in the manufacturing and industrial sectors. Among these were studies on women in electronics factories in St Lucia (Kelly 1986), on women in the garment industry in Belize (BOWAND 1994), on women workers in enclave industries in the OECS (Greene 1990), and on Barbadian women in the manufacturing sector (Massiah 1998). These studies produced concrete data and sometimes startling information about the conditions under which women were employed and worked. They also provided valuable insights into their experiences of working in the factories and of the negative effects on their self-esteem and well-being. All of the studies examined how workers were recruited, their working conditions, wages, health and safety standards, and industrial relations.

Recruitment policies

The recruitment policies and practices of enterprises in the manufacturing and industrial sectors in Caribbean countries are based on the managers' perceptions of women's traditional occupations, like sewing, and on their beliefs about women's inborn natural characteristics like neatness, attention to detail and perseverance. The following statements from male managers are evidence that, as in other sectors of the economy, perceptions and prevailing gender stereotypes continue to dictate and reinforce the gender division in the manufacturing and industrial sectors.

Women are better suited.

Women enjoy routine work and they like doing the same thing over and over.

Their fingers are nimble and better able to do fine and delicate work.

Sewing is a skill inborn in women.

Men are more used to heavy work and find light work too slow.

Women like to work with their hands and to do handicraft; they are more dexterous.

These beliefs, along with awareness of the fact there are large numbers of unemployed women in urgent need of jobs, many of them willing to work for the low wages offered, set the guidelines for prevailing recruitment policies and practices within these sectors.

Women are therefore not generally recruited through existing employment agencies but rather through direct contacts like relatives and friends of current employees. Research has shown that although some factories prefer to recruit older women because 'they are more stable and don't get pregnant', the majority preferred to employ younger women from rural areas rather than urban areas because they believed that the former would be more adaptable and would have better work attitudes. These younger women with some formal basic education are reluctant to work in agriculture, and often see a job in a factory as providing them with higher wages and status and with some opportunity for upward mobility. Even if they are seen as suitable, however, anti-union policies will lead recruitment officers in the factories to quiz prospective workers, before hiring them, about whether they are likely to become union members.

You can't be too old or too tired and you can't get pregnant or they will fire you.

Like their counterparts in other developing countries, women who work in these sectors usually only have a primary education and few if any skills, and are usually engaged in jobs that require minimal skills and little knowledge of the technical aspects of production, and are classified as unskilled or semi-skilled. Once recruited the workers are put on probation, sometimes for as long as a year, during which they may be exposed to short periods of training and be paid a low minimum wage. They have little if any job security and may be fired at any time without notice or benefits; if rehired, they have to start at a lower level for a lower wage. This has been the experience of some electronic factory workers in St Lucia.

When the owners in America have a shortage of work, they send you home for a long time. They then employ new people instead of you. You must try going back, but you are no longer entitled to benefits like holiday pay because they don't consider you an old worker. You must start at a lower hourly rate. I was at the factory for two years and I worked up to supervisor. When I got laid off for two years, I had to start at the quality control level again. (Kelly 1986)

The uncertainty of waiting to be rehired not only prevents these women from exploring other options, but affects their ability to meet their financial needs and those of their families.

They wait until late on the last day of the pay period and then fire you so you lose the next two weeks pay.

Recruitment, hiring and firing practices such as these create an environment within which women's time and labour are exploited; their low self-esteem is further eroded and their livelihoods constantly threatened.

Working conditions

All the research studies and testimonies of women employed in these sectors highlight the undesirable conditions under which women in industrial enclaves and in factories work. Working hours are long and breaks are short. Sometimes as little as half an hour is allowed for lunch and in several of the factory shells toilet and other facilities are limited and inadequate. Lighting is poor. First-aid kits, canteens and lunch rooms are non-existent. Often workers can be seen eating lunch under trees. In many factories, if there was to be a fire the workers would be trapped.

There are so many of us packed in here and the fire door is locked.

In several factories equipment is outdated and unsafe and little protective clothing or gear is provided or required. The absence of proper facilities and appropriate health and safety measures, and of legislation to enforce their provision, means that the workers are often exposed to the effects of harmful chemicals and industrial gases. This has serious implications for their health and safety, and female workers in these factories, like the women who participated in the Kelly study (1986) and in the Massiah study (1991), suffered a wide range of health problems including physical discomfort, eye strain, severe headaches, burns, skin rashes, swollen and broken skin, dizziness, backaches and stress. However, because of their low wages, because they were not covered by health insurance and because they were not paid if they took sick leave, many of them were unable to afford proper treatment for their ailments or to buy glasses or protective clothing.

Women in these factories must work long hours, including overtime without compensation. They are usually given piecework and expected to produce large quantities at high speeds with few mistakes. The work is repetitive, with few if any opportunities to use initiative or creativity and little chance of promotion.

> *I am supposed to do seven big bundles of bras an hour. My job is to sew on one strap. I didn't make my quota as I was feeling sick so I have to work all day instead of half on Saturday to make it up.*

> *Last week the needle went right through my fingernail, but you can't use a thimble, it would hold you back.*

In addition, many women work for as little as US$14.24 per week and deductions are made from wages for latecoming and for mistakes.

> *The minimum wage just covers the basic foodstuff for the children, you have to do a lot of extra work to pay bus fare and the bills.*

Cheap female labour is obviously an important factor that influences the decision of offshore factories to set up shop in the Caribbean. This is reflected in the opinion of several managers who explained that:

> *Most industries have their eyes on the ladies because they are paid less.* (Kelly 1986)

In spite of evidence to the contrary, the rationale for paying women less is still being linked to the perception and belief that women are secondary wage earners, that they are more willing to work for and accept lower wages than men are, and that the work that they do is less valuable than that of men. But while the women who work in these factories know that their labour is worth more, many of them are sole breadwinners who have few other options.

> *Men won't want that low salary, the companies know that they can bluff women.*

> *Yes the pay is too low, but it is a job and because of the kids I have to do it.*

I don't like doing factory work, but I can't stay home or look for another job, so I try to forget the bad side.

In describing the conditions under which they work, many women also said that they were harassed and exploited by managers and some were actually happy when they were fired or when the factories closed down. However, the fear of being unable to feed and provide for their children is often the main reason why so many women remain in these jobs and put up with the poor conditions under which they have to work.

Industrial relations

In the late 1990s, as part of a programme of Women and Work, the Belize Organization for Women and Development (BOWAND) undertook a survey in seven garment factories with the intention of documenting the conditions under which women in the garment-producing factories worked and to highlight the need for greater protection of the rights of the women employed in the industry. The research was undertaken by a woman who was a former employee in one of the factories.

What rights do female factory workers have?

In 1973 a factory called BELGAR was established and hired 100 workers, mostly young women from surrounding villages who had just left school. I was one of those women. After a short period of training we started to sew garments. We did not get paid at the time of training, only after production started. We were paid by the hour, 36 cents per hour or $17.50 per week (Belizean dollars).

When there were problems some of the workers would go to the Labour Department, but would get a deaf ear. There was no social security at the time, the Labour Department was not much help and we had no one to turn to. We had to put up with many things and we had no protection. Many of us just had to go on working because there were no other jobs.

Management took advantage of the workers' fears. Once when the Labour Department took a poll of the workers to see if they wanted it to step in, the manager gave a party for the workers and promised them a lot of things, so the workers turned against the Department and voted with the manager because they were afraid to lose their jobs. They knew that labour laws had not been implemented in the factory, that they had no rights and no protection, that the manager could do what he liked with the workers, and that if the manager discovered that they had voted against him, he would not keep the promises that he had made. Needless to say, after the vote had gone in his favour the manager forgot all about the promises that he had made to the workers.

The factory closed down in 1980.

In 1990 another textile factor opened in Belmopan and I was among the 170, mostly female employees. Wages were still low at $1.25 per hour. I worked as a supervisor. It was very hard. We used to work late into the night without no overtime or time-and-a-half. We complained and were told by the Labour Department that we should be satisfied with what we were getting and that we should be glad to have a job at all.

After a few months we women workers began to voice our opinions. We asked for a piece rate system instead of an hourly rate so as to get compensated for all the work we were doing. The manager agreed but continued to pay us the flat rate of $56.00. We got real angry and decided to join a union. On advice from the Public Service Union we formed our own union, the Women Workers' Union, and I was elected vice-president.

A few days after the manager heard about the union, the executive and a few other women were terminated. The firings made the women even angrier and they closed down all the machines and demanded an explanation for the firings. Instead of giving an explanation the police were called in. The factory was closed and we went on strike. For four months we picketed the factory. Our demands were to be paid by piece rate instead of a flat rate, to rehire all the women who had supported the union, and that management recognize the right of the union to negotiate on behalf of the workers.

➤ During the strike we visited the Labour Office, the Prime Minister's Office and the Ministry of Economic Development almost every day, but we never got a good response. Finally a Board of Inquiry was set up by government and the management of the factory was forced to pay the women back-pay and to rehire the workers who had been fired. However the Board did not require management to recognize the union. Instead, government appointed an intermediary to act as a go-between. The factory was reopened but the workers no longer felt confident and they resented the pressure from the intermediary to accept management conditions. Eventually the women left. Government withdrew the concessions and the factory closed.

Women employed in the garment industry throughout the region experience situations similar to those of the women in Belize. The comments from women working in the manufacturing sector in Barbados who were interviewed in the Massiah study confirm this.

When you do not join a union you have to take whatever they do or say and this is what they like. Once you join a union they get rid of you one way or another.

When the girls started to join a union things started to seem 'a bit slow'. Like they do not want you to join a union. Then you get a lot of hassle from the boss man.

Many of the factories in industrial enclaves are drawn to the Caribbean on the assumption of the availability of cheap female labour, and by concessions given by governments, one of which is that the workers will not become unionized. The experience of the women in the textile factories in Belize and in the manufacturing sector in Barbados, is an indication of the blatant disregard for women's rights as workers and for their right to free association and to join unions. It also overturns the image of female industrial workers as passive and docile.

The public and private sectors

In all countries there are significant numbers of women employed by government in the public services and, as Table 2.7 shows, in most of the countries female civil servants outnumber their male counterparts.

However, data from the 1990–1 census reveal that there has been an increase in the number of women in administrative and in upper and middle management positions, some of whom are permanent sec-retaries and heads of departments in the public services, and that in a few countries there are more women who hold senior administrative and managerial positions than there are men. Figures from the 1991 censuses show that in Dominica about one third of top civil service positions were held by women, while in St Lucia 57 per cent of senior officials, managers and legislators were women. Across the public services as a whole in the same country women also held 50 per cent

Table 2.7 Persons employed in the civil service

Countries	Males (% of employed population)	Females (% of employed population)
Antigua/Barbuda	19.8	16.5
Bahamas	64.6	66
Barbados	22.9	23.1
Belize	13.7	23.4
British Virgin Islands	13.6	13.2
Dominica	10.5	7.9
Grenada	20.1	27.7
Guyana	31.2	44.2
Montserrat	24.3	31.6
St Kitts–Nevis	32.3	26.6
St Lucia	13.2	16.7
St Vincent & the Grenadines	17.1	26.4
Trinidad & Tobago	39.3	35.3

Source: Mondesire & Dunn (1997).

Table 2.8 Males and females employed in the private sector

Country	Males (% of employed population)	Females (% of employed population)
Antigua/Barbuda	40.3	33.4
Bahamas	19.1	24.9
Barbados	38.5	38.5
Belize	52.8	57.4
British Virgin Islands	55.1	49.2
Dominica	28.3	17.3
Grenada	42.4	43.2
Guyana	35.6	29.6
Montserrat	54.1	56.1
St Kitts—Nevis	48.2	57.2
St Lucia	50.6	56.1
St Vincent & the Grenadines	53.3	51.2
Trinidad & Tobago	36.8	50.3

Source: Mondesire and Dunn (1997).

of the jobs. Yet in spite of this the majority of female civil servants still occupy lower-level, low-status positions in such traditional female occupations as secretaries, typists and clerks.

Within the private sector in seven Caribbean countries, there were more female employees than there were males. However, while there is probably more opportunity for upward mobility within private companies, and while in several countries the number of women in senior management positions has increased and more women have managed to 'storm the bastions of male power', the glass ceiling is still securely in place and women are still conspicuously absent from the majority of board rooms across the region.

The informal sector

There are large numbers of women who operate in the informal sector of Caribbean economies who manage successful businesses and who are making a significant contribution to the development of many small and medium enterprises (SMEs). They operate as entrepreneurs, petty traders, hairdressers, seamstresses, handicraft makers, shopkeepers, owners of restaurants, small eating places, and day-care centres, and as traders in commercial goods.

Recent research by the International Labour Organization (ILO) has shown that women are a significant percentage of those employed in this sector. In Barbados and Grenada there are more women in the informal than in the formal sectors of the economy. In Jamaica, about 50 per cent of those employed in this sector are women; in Trinidad and Tobago, 36.1 per cent; in Guyana, just over a third (34.8 per cent). In Dominica in 1992, half of the businesses were registered to women; and in Belize, too, large numbers of women are engaged in wholesale and/or retail businesses. In several countries significant numbers of women own businesses that they have started from their own savings, often accumulated through informal su su, box or meeting turn schemes, or with money borrowed from relatives. However, it is important to identify where these women are located within the sector; the nature, type and size of their businesses; the constraints that they face; and the factors that have contributed to their success or failure.

The women in this sector are often those who have been unable to find employment in the formal sectors, either because of the unavailability of jobs or because they have few marketable skills and are therefore not qualified to fill jobs that do exist. Women are concentrated in the retail trade, selling clothes, cosmetics, craft goods and food; many are engaged in catering and in food preservation, processing and preparation. There are also a significant number of female artisans like hairdressers, seamstresses and craft makers. A growing number of female entrepreneurs are venturing into non-traditional areas once considered to be male, and establishing successful micro and medium-sized businesses in such fields as woodwork and small appliance repairs.

While for large numbers of women working in the informal sector is their only means of income, a number of employed women are also engaged in economic activities in the informal sector to generate additional income. The activities and experiences in which each of these groups is engaged may be significantly different.

The first group is usually made up of poor, unemployed women from low-income rural and urban communities. They are mostly involved in selling agricultural produce, food, clothing, household articles and other sundry items. They lack working capital and have little if any access to credit; they do not undertake market research and have little or no access to formal training in business management. As a result the market is overcrowded with hundreds of women, many of whom can be seen on pavements throughout the region, selling the same things and getting little profit.

Yet as sales and opportunities for expansion increase some of these women are able to expand their business and offer a wider variety of merchandise, mainly through the 'barrel trade'. This trade is a thriving business through which several women may either receive articles from relatives abroad or may travel to identify and purchase new lines of goods in North America and Venezuela to sell from stalls or on pavements along the road. This has led to the creation of 'bend down plazas' throughout the region, so called because customers often have to 'bend down' to select articles from the pavement. These informal commercial importers have emerged as an organized and vibrant group in Jamaica; and while women on some of the other islands may not be as well organized, they are in the same business.

The informal commercial importers in Jamaica, the hucksters and pavement vendors on all islands selling everything from cosmetics and clothes to small household appliances, and middle-class/professional women who travel to North America and bring back merchandise to sell to their co-workers, family and friends – all are an important part of the informal or alternative economy in the region. These women manage micro, small and medium-sized businesses and, according to

The Caribbean Association of Women Entrepreneurs (CAWE)

The Caribbean Association of Women Entrepreneurs was founded in 1998 as a result of the Mega Market 98. The Mega Market was, and is, a forum organized by CAWE to provide opportunities for women who own and operate businesses to expose their goods, products and services to regional and international business people, and thus to expand their markets. It also encourages and facilitates networking among female entrepreneurs from across the region and provides them with support.

CAWE's goal is to provide opportunities for women who own and operate businesses so that they will be able to fulfil their potential, access wider markets, and successfully operate and sustain the growth and development of their businesses.

Among CAWE's activities are conferences, exhibitions, networking and support services to its members, mentoring of young entrepreneurs, and activities to increase the visibility of women entrepreneurs.

the ILO, are estimated to account for between 35 and 50 per cent of the small enterprise sector across the region.

Another well-organized group operating in the informal sector are the hucksters, of whom about 80–90 per cent are women. These women are mainly involved in transporting and selling agricultural produce within their own countries and in other countries throughout the region. Many of them travel on a weekly basis to other islands to sell their produce, either in the open market or to regular clients.

Several professional women also operate in this sector but, unlike their unemployed counterparts, they are often able to access credit from banks and to invest capital into their additional economic activities. Their clientele is also often more clearly defined and select, and they are not as vulnerable to shifting market forces as their poorer counterparts. Their businesses are probably better managed as they have acquired and are able to apply more technical skills and professional approaches. However, while they definitely see their activities in the informal sector as an important source of additional income, many may not regard them as businesses in the strictest sense.

Because of the increase in the number of women who own small and medium-sized businesses in the informal sector more attention is gradually being paid to female entrepreneurs, including attempts to provide them with resources, technical assistance and support. The National Development Foundations (NDFs) organize training and provide technical assistance to female entrepreneurs on an ongoing basis and some National Machineries for the Advancement of Women do the same. In 2000 the Department of Gender Affairs in Trinidad and Tobago organized a breakfast seminar for middle-income business-women in which participants identified their practical and longer-term needs and strategies for meeting them. A new regional organization, the Caribbean Association of Women Entrepreneurs (CAWE), has also recently been formed to focus on the needs of women entrepreneurs.

Women in non-traditional occupations

While significant numbers of women participate in the labour force, research has shown that although there has been an increase in the number of women in non-traditional 'male' occupations, they still predominate in traditional female occupations. For example, in Trinidad and Tobago in 1997 female participation in construction was less than 3 per cent. At the same time 'male' occupations that require technical and vocational skills are in great demand, are more highly remunerated, and are awarded higher status than occupations in the services sector where women predominate. Over the last two decades an increasing number of women have sought to acquire technical and vocational skills in non-traditional areas, mainly in the construction industry and in electrical repairs and electronics. A small number have gained employment in private companies, but an increasing number have established their own businesses.

The incentive for women to move into these non-traditional areas of work has grown with the understanding and recognition that women not only have the ability to acquire and use skills that were once thought to be 'natural' for men, but that they have the right to pursue work and occupations of their choice. Research has also shown that confining women to a narrow range of female career choices and options effectively excludes them from lucrative sectors of the labour market.

During the 1980s and 1990s a number of research studies examined and analysed female participation in existing technical and vocational education and training programmes, the subjects to which they were being exposed, their career aspirations and their attitudes towards non-traditional work. Among these was a CARICOM regional study in 1988 on the Participation of Women in Technical and Vocational Education and Training, a study on Attitudes Towards Non-traditional Work among Grenadian Women (Gittens and Manigo 1986) and an Employment Training Survey (ACCA 1986).

Data from these studies not only revealed that girls were choosing 'female subjects' but that there was still a deep-rooted belief among male and female students and tutors, as well as among employers and the wider society, that females were incapable of and/or unfit for 'men's work'. Some tutors in technical and vocational institutions did and still do believe that subjects such as motor mechanics, carpentry and metal work are unfeminine, while others are convinced that girls are afraid of machinery and tools, and unable to lift 'heavy machinery'.

During the 1980s, too, a number of programmes were organized in several countries to train women and girls in non-traditional skills. In 1985, as part of its continuing education programme the Ministry of Education in Grenada developed a project to train unemployed young women in non-traditional areas of work including meter reading, pipe fitting, refrigeration and motor mechanics. One year later, the Division of Women's Affairs in Grenada implemented a two-year training course for women in motor mechanics and the Bureau of Women's Affairs in Jamaica implemented a training programme in apiculture and small-appliance repairs for women. At the same time, some technical and vocational institutes began to offer courses and programmes for women and to expose them to the construction trades and other traditional male trades. In addition to the initiatives of the

National Machinery for the Advancement of Women and educational institutions, various NGOs in several countries also organized non-formal training programmes for women in a variety of non-traditional areas including woodwork, repairs of electrical appliances, car maintenance, carpentry, masonry and plumbing.

The St Andrews Woodwork Project in Grenada and the Women's Constructive Collective in Jamaica are examples of initiatives that successfully trained unemployed women in non-traditional skills. The former was implemented by CANSAVE in a rural community in Grenada in the 1980s; it trained young adults and parents in carpentry and woodwork so that they could make furniture and toys for the pre-school. The Women's Collective trained unemployed women from a low-income urban community in Kingston, Jamaica in basic construction skills. Participants in the project not only learnt technical skills in carpentry, masonry and reading blueprints, but they also developed skills in small business management and accounting. These became important when the Collective became a company in 1985 and a team of three had to assume responsibility for its management. Because of the training received, the members of the Collective were initially able to find employment on construction sites and later to operate and manage their own business, to construct small buildings, to manufacture furniture and to do restoration work. In this way they were pioneers and contributed to the erosion of stereotypes held by women as well as men about 'women's work' and 'men's work'.

In spite of these initiatives to train women in non-traditional skills, several women who were exposed to training and who acquired non-traditional skills initially found it difficult to obtain jobs. For example, the woman who topped the class in a motor mechanics course in Grenada was only able to get a job in the machine shop as a clerk. Moreover, the Employment Training Survey referred to earlier found that 10 per cent of the firms interviewed were of the view that females were not suited to certain occupations because of physical demands, and that over 80 per cent employed fewer than five women in supervisory positions.

As a result of these early initiatives and of the growing awareness and changing perceptions about women's roles, an increasing number of women are not only being employed in non-traditional occupations but several have started and developed successful businesses in areas such as woodwork, repairs of small appliances, manufacturing and distribution of industrial gases. Like their counterparts in the SMEs and the informal sector, however, many of these women face a number of constraints: the demands of their reproductive roles; social and cultural barriers that perpetuate negative attitudes towards women; the gender division of labour; and insufficient access to credit, land, technology and support services.

Between 1999 and 2000 a study on women in the construction sector in Antigua and Barbuda surveyed 31 female respondents, including girls in secondary schools who were receiving or had received formal training in building technology and women employed in the construction industry (Parris 2000). Data from this study revealed that the majority of the respondents were of the view that formal training in building technology had increased their career options and employability. However, they also felt that while opportunities are now available for females to receive training and acquire skills in construction trades, parents do not encourage their daughters to study building technology and females are unaware of the range of possible careers within the industry, including civil engineering and architecture. They also indicated that because of the poor image and low social status of construction workers, and the 'male culture' of construction sites, few females are attracted to these jobs or show an interest in choosing construction as a career.

CHAPTER 3

Women in Leadership and Decision Making

While males continue to hold the majority of senior and managerial positions, in recent years a significantly higher number of women have moved up to legislative, senior and managerial positions in the public sector and to a lesser extent in the private sector.

However, there are still only a small number of women who hold or have held positions of leadership at the highest levels of Caribbean society. In the last 25 years, while there has been only one female prime minister, Dame Eugenia Charles of Dominica, there have been a few female governor-generals: the late Dame Nita Barrow of Barbados, and Dame Pearette Louisy and Dame Minta Gordon, current holders of the office in St Lucia and Belize respectively. There have also been female attorney-generals in St Lucia and Barbados, for example, and labour commissioners in Barbados, St Kitts, and the Turks and Caicos Islands. In Barbados the cabinet secretary and the governor of the central bank, and in St Vincent the chief personnel officer and the clerk of parliament are women. In several countries there are also a number of women who hold the position of permanent secretary.

In the private sector, few women are CEOs or chairpersons of boards. In 1993 only four (5 per cent) of the 75 companies that were members of the Trinidad and Tobago Manufacturers' Association had women who were executive heads, while 15 (20 per cent) had female sales managers.

Women's reluctance to seek and accept leadership positions in organizations is often attributed to the amount of time and effort required to function in these positions, to the pressure to which individuals in these positions are subjected, and to the challenges women would face in juggling their reproductive, productive and civic roles. While this may be true in some cases, it has also been recognized that social norms and attitudes, structural and behavioural factors, and top-down approaches to decision making and management create barriers that limit female participation and involvement in leadership positions in organizations.

Political involvement

Over the last few years there have been several calls for larger numbers of women in the region to become more actively involved in politics, and for them to be elected to positions of leadership and power at the highest levels of policy and decision making. Women themselves have begun to pay more attention to this issue and to discuss its implications for them as women, for their countries and for the region. They have also begun to explore ways in which they can transform politics and political practices so as to make politics more humane and people-centred, and less corrupt.

Women's involvement in political processes does not begin and end with national parliaments and senates, but extends to important public institutions and agencies that shape national policy. Statutory boards, commissions of enquiry, foreign embassies, trade unions and political parties provide women with opportunities to participate at the highest levels of policy formulation and decision making, and to influence the direction of national life.

Although over the last quarter century more women have become actively involved in political processes, and today are playing leadership roles in decision making and management, in many cases high-flying women remain implementers rather than shapers of decisions and policy. Women also remain under-represented at the highest levels in trade unions, political parties and senior government policy-making positions, and few countries have set specific targets for increasing the number of women in parliament or the senate.

In very few Caribbean countries, therefore, do women participate equally with men at the highest levels in politics, whether in leadership positions in political parties, as elected members of parliament or as ministers of government and senators. Consequently, women's voices are conspicuously absent from political and parliamentary debates and it is unusual for either women's needs and concerns or issues of gender equality to be taken into consideration when national policies are being formulated and national budgets are being developed.

Women's low participation in politics is influenced by several factors, including their negative perceptions of politics as dirty and corrupt, the gender division of labour within trade unions and political parties (denying them the opportunity to hold leadership positions within these organizations), their lack of access to funds to contest elections and to campaign, their inability to mobilize and build a constituency of women, and the lack of support of female voters. In addition, there appears to be some tension between older and younger women in political institutions and leadership positions: women parliamentarians are seldom celebrated as leaders or regarded as role models to inspire younger women to choose careers in politics. In some countries there are women whose success in politics appears to have been influenced by family tradition. For these women this route seemed inevitable: their fathers or other male relatives had been important political figures and this legacy grants visibility, confidence and electoral momentum. While this is not and should not be the only or the most important criterion for judging the political careers of these women, along with class it is an important factor that influences people's attitudes and ultimately their acceptance of these women in the political arena. Consequently, because of who they are and where they come from, these women have a distinct advantage over women who do not have a dynastic tradition of family political involvement.

Since 1981 the electoral office in Barbados has compiled electoral data to reflect gender characteristics and the data show that between 6 and 8 per cent more women registered to vote than did men, and that on average women would have an advantage of about 400 votes over men in most of the constituencies. Since 1981, too, 69 per cent of the women registered to vote actually voted as compared with 65 per cent of the men. Consequently, while the numbers of women holding political office are not large, women as voters do hold power to influence the political process. However, women themselves seem not to realize that as a group they do hold this power, that through more active participation in the political process they can ensure the election of more women to parliament, and that they can demand better represention of women and their involvement at the highest levels of policy and decision making.

Trade unions

Historically, because of patriarchy and well-entrenched male dominance, women in trade unions have had and continue to have low status. They are regarded merely as members and under-represented in leadership and executive positions, and this is so even in teachers' unions in which there are larger numbers of female than of male members. In Trinidad and Tobago, 26,770 or 44 per cent of the members in 28 trade unions were women, but only 15 women in eight unions held executive positions. These women together represent 7.6 per cent of all executive positions. Most blatantly, in two unions in which more than half of the members were women, no woman held an executive position (Trinidad and Tobago 1995).

In the Barbados Workers Union, the largest and possibly the most powerful union in the country, only five of the 24-member executive council are women. In a study to evaluate the status of women in this union (Barrow 1996), women who were interviewed saw their role as being supportive, expressed the view that being on the executive was a 'man's thing', described leadership as being 'too political', and saw politics as 'a dirty game' in which they were reluctant to participate. In addition, 80 per cent of them said that they would never run for the position of general secretary because they didn't 'have the qualities to be a good general secretary', and believed that women could bring about more change by 'making noise from the floor' (*ibid.*: 22). On the other hand, those women who said that they would be willing to run for the post of senual secretary said that it was a hard task, that neither they nor the union were yet ready for a female general secretary, and that if they ran they would not get 'a high level of support from the women'. Male interviewers also felt that women were not, and might never be, ready for top leadership positions (*ibid.*: 23).

Before the 1970s trade unions paid little attention to the specific needs and concerns of female workers or members, but during the last two decades several initiatives have been taken to increase awareness about the need for unions to put women's issues and, later, gender issues on their agendas. In the 1980s, regional and national programmes were organized to sensitize female members of trade unions about the trade union movement, to increase their understanding about how power is distributed and used in unions, to train them for leadership and to motivate them to access positions of power in their unions and within the movement. In the early 1980s WAND and the Trade Union Institute on the Mona campus of UWI implemented comprehensive training for female members of unions from countries across the region. Following this, trade unions in several countries implemented programmes for their female members. The Joint Trade Unions' Research and Development Centre (JTURDC) in Jamaica also organized a programme designed to train women to access higher positions in the trade union movement.

As female members of trade unions began to show an interest in union business and to stress the need for their unions to begin to pay attention to the needs of female workers and members, some unions appointed a member of the executive committee, invariably male, to be responsible for women's issues. But gradually unions began to put structures and mechanisms in place to meet the needs of female workers, to address women's issues and to integrate a gender perspective into their work. They set up women's committees, and more recently gender committees. However, while in some unions, the general feeling of the executive committee members was that the women's committees' main responsibility was to raise funds, the women in these committees saw them as having a wider role and a responsibility to develop and implement programmes to address women's concerns and issues.

The union did not address women's issues, an executive member was responsible for women's affairs but nothing happened.

The women's movement influenced me to set up a women's committee in my union.

According to women in one union in Dominica, the creation of a separate women's committee within the union was a positive step that led to some change. Since its formation, women's issues have been integrated into the union's overall programme, and female members have been motivated to become more involved in union business.

There has been a change since the women's committee was set up. The committee has its own executive and draws up its own programme. Women see themselves as people to make change, are more involved in the union, and have their own sessions. The committee also sees the importance of joining with other social partners to address women's issues.

On the other hand there have been some negative responses and reactions from male members in this union.

They say that there are too many feminists in the trade union movement.

They find subtle ways and means to bring down the women.

In spite of the negative attitudes and reactions of some male members, some unions are attempting to address the concerns and meet the needs of their female members. Some have implemented a wide variety of education and training programmes to sensitize members about women's issues and about gender, and to train women in specific areas of union business, for example in industrial relations and bargaining. While these initiatives have introduced a gender perspective into many unions it is clear that as yet women, women's issues and gender issues have not been integrated fully into the unions' business at the level of policy and decision making, For example, in spite of the growing concern about sexual harassment in the workplace in several countries, unions have not agitated aggressively for legislation on this and it does not appear to be one of their priorities. At the same time, even though women may want to push women's issues, they have to work with men who are still at the top of the union and who don't see these as important.

Another indication that women are still not accepted as leaders or represented at the upper echelons of trade unions is their absence on platforms and as keynote speakers at trade union conferences. In these fora, while a token woman may be on the platform, she is usually given the task of either saying the prayers, reading the Bible lesson or giving the vote of thanks. Few if any women are ever given the opportunity to make a speech, or to advance their views on what is seen as an important issue. Moreover, a woman who attempts to intervene at this level is often deliberately pushed into the background and ignored.

Profile of Ms D

I became involved in the trade union because my goal was to improve the position of working-class people. I have been in the union for over 25 years and over that period I moved from the administrative section into the 'belly' of the union. I joined in the mid-1970s when there was a lot happening in the women's movement but in the union women were not in leadership, and as a women I felt that women had a greater role to play.

Trade unionism was and still is a male-dominated area and women have had to fight to get any real voice within the leadership structure. Although there were women in the union who were well qualified academically, we knew almost nothing about trade unionism. Participation in the Caribbean Women in Trade Unions Project provided an opportunity to study trade unionism as well as Women in Development, and helped women to realize that they had the potential to assume leadership positions in their unions.

The male head of my union was adamant that he didn't have a men's group and that there was no need for a women's group in the union or for me to be doing these studies. There was a lot of objection from the men but I was passionate and determined to show the men that we women could do it. There was also a lot of backlash aimed at preventing women from reaching the top, at showing who was in control, and at emphasizing that anytime women got out of hand or got the wrong impression they would be put 'back in their place'.

For example I was shifted from position to position. They made sure that if I could do something well, I would be moved to a new position and would always have to start over. Even the position that I hold now, I was put into it to kill the momentum that I had developed in another area that is an important part of the union's programme, and that I had the mettle to do. This wears you out. It takes away your energy from where you are focusing it to reach the top, and you constantly have to catch up to get back to where you were before. It has caused me to constantly evaluate, re-evaluate and reflect on myself.

When women do get into leadership positions they find it difficult to deal with women's issues as they might want. I continued to organize sessions with other women to deal with women's issues, but I have been taken out of the mainstream planning because it is felt that I indoctrinate women into being against men. I did get support from a few men, not because I was addressing women's issues, but because they saw me as being strong and enjoyed sparring with me.

Previously there was a women's sub-committee and while it has its own programmes and does deal with some women's issues it does not challenge the established norms, and the individuals chosen or appointed to it would not be expected to do so. I do not feel that the union has addressed women's issues or workers' issues from a woman's perspective, as issues like maternity leave are regarded as a worker's issue and seen as part of the general work of trade unions.

The recent emphasis on gender has provided a 'way out' of dealing with women's issues and the male leaders use this to rationalize their approach of dealing with people, rather than with either women or men exclusively. They see women who want to deal with women's issues as backward and narrow. I don't think that women have found their niche yet.

While more women in trade unions are now more aware and conscious of the need for trade unions to address the needs of female members and workers, many are still not inclined to raise these issues or to agitate for them to be included in the union's agenda. They feel that if they did this they would be seen as radical and branded as being cantankerous, arrogant and 'unladylike'.

> I think that we have gone backwards. In the 1980s we had vibrant discussions, we would argue and agitate about a number of things. Nowadays, if you do this in a meeting, everybody looks at you and says, 'What's wrong with you, why are you being so aggressive?'

The political parties

Political parties are the training ground for future parliamentarians. Election to and acceptance of leadership positions, and active participation in the running of the party, provide opportunities for members to gain the knowledge and skills required to compete successfully in national elections. In most political parties women are regarded as the 'backbone' of the party and there is either a women's 'arm', women's auxiliary, women's league, women's wing or women's committee. However, in some parties the women's 'arm' is not an autonomous body, does not have its own constitution, does not pay special attention to women's issues and does not actively seek to create and build a constituency of women or to promote and strategize vigorously to ensure that women are elected to positions of leadership in the party, and selected to contest national elections.

Few women are elected to or hold leadership positions in political parties, and while in some parties one of the vice-presidents is usually a woman, the majority of female members do not participate actively or become intimately involved in 'party business'. Nor do the few women who are appointed or selected for top positions always receive the support of female members of the party.

On the whole, the women's groups within political parties continue to be supportive of male members, preparing the ground for elections and raising funds. Very few, if any special attempts are made by them to promote and facilitate greater participation of female members in politics or to prepare and equip them for active participation in the political processes in the party or in the country. Neither do women's groups nor women in political parties organize themselves or build constituencies of women so that they are able to demand that women candidates be placed in constituencies that are seen as important or as safe seats, and in which they have greater chances of winning.

Prospective female candidates are also seldom proactive and are therefore more likely to take what is offered to them and to accept constituencies in which they know they are unlikely to win the seat. The lingering perception that women should not be out there rubbing shoulders with male candidates has also had a strong influence on branch members, including female members. Faced with prospective male and female candidates, more often than not they will nominate and support the man rather than the woman.

I know a woman who is doing a lot of ground work and is positioning herself with the hope of being chosen to represent the constituency, but she is no further along and people in the constituency as well as branch members will probably select the man as their candidate.

In a recent election in one country, an attempt was made by women in one of the parties contesting the elections to create a 'women's platform' as part of the campaign strategy, to draw attention to and discuss women's issues. However their efforts were squashed by the male chairperson of the campaign committee, because in his view this was not necessary and it 'would not bear fruit'. Many male leaders in political parties still do not understand and are unwilling to accept that women's issues are critical to the achievement of national development goals. They, as well as female members of political parties and large numbers of women, also still regard politics as a male domain and see women who aspire to political office and positions of power in the party or at national level as not feminine.

The experience of two women who contested national elections highlight the obstacles and constraints that female candidates face.

Profile of Ms G

Before I became a member of the party I had been doing a lot of work for my representative for many years and when he lost the election I felt that I could make a greater contribution by joining the party. I organized and mobilized people and did everything to motivate people to support the party and very quickly was chosen as chairperson of the branch, but at that time I did not have any desire to be a candidate in the national elections. I worked with women in the women's league, organized seminars and workshops, represented and spoke on behalf of my branch, and gradually began to be seen as a possible candidate.

Eventually I was asked to be a candidate for an urban constituency. I agreed to see what would happen, but I didn't win the nomination from my branch. Later I was asked to run in my own constituency. I was not keen because I knew its history and that it was a stronghold of the rival party, but I felt that it was important to show that women had the potential to be there and that someone should be there representing women.

Facing the electorate I went in full force and did reasonably well. I did not go in with a women's agenda, nor did I try to focus too much on the woman thing. Country people don't look at women's issues, they look at bread and butter issues, at being in the struggle for poor people. That is why I wanted to get into the urban constituency, because I felt that women in town understood women's issues more and that there I would have had the potential to move. When you are representing rural areas your politics have to change. The woman who ran there before me was 'a lady', and I had to say 'I am no lady, I am a woman in here fighting politics. This is no Sunday school.' I am not sure that the party always understands the culture and traditions of different constituencies, especially in terms of the rural/urban divide.

I faced the electorate three times and lost each time to a man. I expected nasty things to be said about me and I took them in my stride. Men seem to be concerned about who they will rub shoulders with in parliament.

➡ I feel that I didn't get the support from the party that was necessary to push me as somebody who might not make it against a strong contender for the other party. They never paid sufficient attention and I had to do a lot on my own. Women don't get into taking money the same way as men and I never approached certain organizations or individuals for financial support, so my financial support would have had to come through the party. You can't be always out there struggling on your own, and the party tended to give financial support to persons, invariably men, who they thought could win their seats.

Profile of Ms T

At the constituency level, women are strong branch members and fiercely loyal to the party. I started as a member of a branch and after a while through a process I moved up to being a committee member, an officer, and finally became chairperson of the branch. But men did not have to go through this process; they could be appointed or elected as officers right away.

In the early years there was a lot of pressure from the men and I always had to be fighting a battle about woman's place. Although the women's league was strong and did a lot of groundwork and campaigning, the party did not have a woman's agenda and women were not encouraged to contest national elections, and as candidates they were not given the support necessary to run a successful campaign or win a seat. Once I wrote a letter asking to be allowed to run for a constituency, but I was refused because I was a woman.

A few years later I was selected to run in a very difficult constituency and I had to develop my own strategy. I focused my attention on the women. I started a women's group and worked with them on different projects designed to teach them skills and to develop their self-esteem, self-confidence and independence. This group became my base, and I did win the seat.

In recent years, some political parties have taken initiatives to increase the participation of women in decision making through their selection for and appointment to positions of leadership. Within the People's National Party in Jamaica a growing concern about the gender imbalance and the absence of females in the leadership of the party led to an initiative to increase the participation of women at this level. In 1998, 700 delegates in Region 3 adopted a gender equity position. Spearheaded by the chairperson of the largest region, and supported by delegates, the initiative resulted in women being elected to contest 16 of the 40 divisions in this region and winning eleven (27.5 per cent) of the seats (Vassell 1999) During the recent conference of the Democrat Labour Party in Barbados, leaders in the party said that they were not interested in tokenism. They pointed out that 30 per cent of the positions in the executive were held by women and that more women had to assume leadership positions within the party.

Women in parliament

Data collected in 1998 reveal that while women held only 16.4 per cent of parliamentary seats, over the last two decades there has been an increase in the number of women elected and appointed to parliamentary assemblies in the region. For example, the number of women in parliament moved from an average of 9.6 per cent in 1980 to 12.6 per cent in 1990, and to 14.66 per cent in 1996 (Vassell 1999). As Table 3.1 shows, more women were nominated (26 per cent) to upper houses or senates than were elected (13 per cent) to lower houses of parliament, and very few women are cabinet members, or are participating at the highest levels of political and national decision making and policy formulation. Overall, men hold well over 80 per cent of elected seats and over 70 per cent of nominated seats; thereby, they continue to dominate and control the political system, retaining executive power and authority as the key decision makers and contributors to national policy.

The few women who are elected to the houses of parliament are not only outnumbered by their male colleagues, but also face several

Table 3.1 Women in parliament and cabinet (1998)

Country	Lower house			Upper house			Cabinet		
	M	F	% F	M	F	% F	M	F	% F
Antigua/Barbuda	18	1	5.2	14	3	17.6	10	0	0
Bahamas	34	6	15	11	5	31.2	10	3	23
Barbados	25	3	10.7	14	7	33	10	3	23
Belize	27	2	6.9	5	4	44.4	15	1	6.25
British Virgin Islands	11	2	15.3	-	-	-	4	2	33
Dominica	18	3	14.2	9	0	0	12	3	20
Grenada	12	3	20	11	2	15.3	11	1	8.3
Guyana	63	12	16	-	-	-	-	-	-
Jamaica	52	8	13	16	5	23.8	15	2	11.7
Montserrat	9	1	10	-	-	-	6	1	14.2
St Kitts–Nevis	13	2	13.3	-	-	-	8	0	0
St Lucia	15	2	11.7	9	2	18	14	2	12.5
St Vincent & the Grenadines	29	1	3.3	-	-	-	12	0	0
Trinidad & Tobago	32	4	11.1	20	11	35.4	20	2	9

Source: Vassell (1999).

constraints that limit their full participation and their ability to ensure that women's concerns and gender issues are addressed. On one hand, women who have been elected to parliament may not be aware of or concerned about gender inequalities or gender equity, or about changing women's position of disadvantage, and therefore may not be committed to taking action to address their issues. On the other hand, they may not be gender sensitive, nor understand the relationship between gender and the process and outcomes of national policies and programmes.

In addition, few women on entering parliament fully understand legislative procedures, or have developed the skills in building alliances, networking and lobbying that are essential for ensuring that critical issues are integrated into and successfully addressed in parliamentary processes.

When you get into parliament there is nobody to teach you anything.

Prevailing gender-biased, negative attitudes and comments of their male colleagues help to undermine female parliamentarians. On occasion these women have been referred to as 'the kitchen cabinet', and 'the petticoat government'. These derogatory names help to reinforce and perpetuate the perception and belief that women are only suited to perform domestic roles, and they draw into question these and other women's ability to handle matters of state.

Profile of Ms L

I was an elected member for one term and a senator for four, but I was never made a minister and although I thought that I was more capable than some of the men who were chosen to be ministers, I never challenged or pushed. I was resentful because I felt that I had been passed over, but I rationalized it the first time around and didn't show my resentment.

I was sorry that I was appointed to the senate as a member of government because I felt that if I had been in the opposition I would have had more opportunity to deal with issues. As a senator you were free only to deal with issues that are on the senate's agenda.

When you get into parliament it is difficult to focus on women's issues when the party has no women's agenda, and if you bring up women's issues it may hamper or bring down the party, so you have no choice, and it is difficult.

Women in local government

Not all countries in the Caribbean have local government structures but where there are such systems, while they are still dominated by men, there are more women at this level than there are in parliament. In Antigua in 1997, 43 (40.9 per cent) of the 102 persons nominated to district councils were women. In the Bahamas 175 women, 22.9 per cent of the candidates, won seats in the first local government elections in 1996. In 1993 in Guyana, 22 per cent of the representatives in the various councils were women. In Jamaica 24 per cent of those elected to serve as councillors were women, and three (23 per cent) of the 13 mayors are women. In Trinidad and Tobago 17 per cent of the councillors are women. In Jamaica the initiative to increase participation of women in local government was taken by the People's National Party within the context of local government elections in 1998. As a result, women were elected to contest 16 of the 40 divisions in the region, and won 27.5 per cent of the seats (Vassell 1999).

Initiatives and strategies for increasing women's participation in politics

During the latter half of the 1980s concern about the low participation of women in politics has resulted in several initiatives being taken to draw attention to the importance of increasing women's participation in politics and political processes, and representation in the formal political structures. In 1996 at the meeting of Commonwealth Ministers with Responsibility for Women's Affairs held in Trinidad and Tobago, it was proposed that 'member countries should be encouraged to achieve a target of no less than 30 per cent of women in decision making in the political, public, and private sectors by the year 2005' (Commonwealth Secretariat 1997).

Since then, governments as well as women's organizations have taken steps to initiate national and regional activities that would increase women's awareness and understanding of politics and to motivate them to participate more actively in political processes, and between 1997 and 1998 several national and regional activities have focused on, examined and promoted more active and greater participation of women in politics. Among these have been activities to increase women's awareness and understanding of political processes and to prepare and equip them for leadership and decision-making positions at the highest levels of policy and decision making, as well as

WOMEN IN LEADERSHIP AND DECISION MAKING · 65

formal strategies for increasing female representation in parliament. Among the latter have been quotas in Jamaica and St Kitts, Alliances for an Electoral Agenda in Belize and Trinidad and Tobago, and a Women's Political Caucus in Jamaica.

Several such activities have also taken place in Trinidad and Tobago. The Women's Platform Coalition, comprised of women from all the political parties contesting the election, acted to increase the number of women and women's organizations in all spheres of political life. In 1995, as a run-up to the general elections, the Coalition issued a leaflet entitled *Ten Points for Power* for adoption by political parties. It also met with political leaders and female candidates and submitted to the prime minister a list of women who were willing to serve in high public office. In 1999 the Network of NGOs for the Advancement of Women launched a non-partisan political initiative to lobby political parties to increase the number of women candidates to contest the local government elections and conducted training for female candidates from all parties contesting the elections. As a result there was an increase in the number of women elected as councillors and appointed as aldermen. The Network subsequently launched a Women's Campaign Fund to support women who wanted to run for political office.

In 1998 the Department of Gender Affairs launched the Women's Leadership and Enhancement Institute to provide training that would increase women's leadership capabilities and prepare them to become more actively involved in political activity. In 2000 the Institute organized a conference on Women in National Leadership: Creating Quality Women Leaders. Its focus was on women in politics and over one hundred women from all political parties participated. Seven women who had been in politics and had served in various national offices – among them a speaker of the House of Representatives, a president of the senate, ministers of government and the founder of a political party – were honoured with awards for their contributions to the political process in the country. The keynote address was given by Dame Eugenia Charles, former prime minister of Dominica and the region's first and only female premier to date, who shared her experiences as party chief, opposition leader and prime minister.

In 2000, a female senator in Trinidad and Tobago strongly expressed the view that women parliamentarians were notably under-represented in the lower house, and that it was important for women to be visible on the slate of those being presented for national elections. She also planned to introduce a private motion to require 'that government and the official opposition join together to pass legislation to ensure that all political parties be required to select the same ratio of women and men as occurs in the population to contest national elections'. She never got the chance to introduce this motion, however, as other issues preceded it and the senate was then adjourned.

In Jamaica the Business and Professional Women's Club created the Women's Political Caucus 'to encourage and facilitate the participation of women in active politics at the highest level and to raise the number of female parliamentarians to at least 40 per cent of the total members of parliament' (Stuart 1998). It provides training for women who are aspiring to political office and in 1995, in collaboration with the Association of Women's Organizations in Jamaica (AWOJ), organized a rally to focus on and discuss women's participation in politics and decision making. Working Women for Transformation, another women's group in Jamaica, has also agitated for a quota system for getting more women into local government.

In Barbados in 1991, the Bureau of Women's Affairs organized a training programme on Civic Education for National Leadership, and in 1997–8 the National Organization of Women implemented a 'Share Power Programme' that involved women from all political parties in a public education and outreach programme. Meetings were held in market squares and female members of political parties spoke of the challenges that they faced in balancing their political involvement with their reproductive and productive roles, while female politicians and parliamentarians spoke of the challenges they faced operating in an area dominated by men, and appealed for solidarity and support from women. In 2000 the UWI School of Continuing Studies ran a three-month course on Women in Politics. The 18 women who participated were exposed to lectures and panel discussions on topics including possibilities for women in politics, gender relations and politics, the structure of government, estimates and budgetary proposals, women's leadership, protocol and etiquette in the public service, effective political presentations, parliamentary procedures and women in comparative political systems.

In 1998 the United Nations Development Programme (UNDP) provided support to the government of Guyana for a project entitled Building Capacity for Gender Equity in Governance. The project sought to enhance the role of women in decision making and to facilitate their informed and effective participation in community, government, political and civil organizations. One of the outcomes of this project was the establishment of the Guyana Women's Leadership Institute with the responsibility for designing and implementing appropriate leadership programmes for women and girls. The Institute has organized a number of activities and training programmes for various groups of women, including a National Amerindian Women's Conference to examine and discuss the position and status of Amerindian women, and their low participation and representation in the formal political structures.

This account of various initiatives in different countries of the region is far from exhaustive. In Belize, for example, the Women's Agenda has developed a civil society agenda and a strategy for placing women in 30 per cent of the positions on public boards (see Figure 3.1). In St Lucia, a recent conference with a similar focus examined women's role in local government.

There have also been significant initiatives at a region-wide level. A regional meeting organized by government in collaboration with NGOs was held in Trinidad in 1998 to discuss Women in Power and Decision Making. The participants, women activists and leaders, shared their experiences of leadership, power and constituency building, and reviewed and discussed women's participation in political processes. At the end of the meeting the Caribbean sub-regional branch of the Global Network of Women in Politics was launched.

In 1998 CAFRA and the Women's Forum of Barbados organized a regional round table dialogue on Women in Politics. This activity brought together women politicians, parliamentary representatives, members of political parties, trade unions, women's organizations, youth groups, activists and members of the media from several countries. Discussions focused on how women can broaden their vision of politics and act collectively as catalysts to transform the nature and practice of politics (Thorne 1998).

Later in 1998 a regional symposium on Gender, Politics, Peace and Conflict was attended by male and female parliamentarians from 14 Commonwealth Caribbean countries. The participants identified the need to train female politicians, including party members, candidates and parliamentary representatives. They also developed strategies for engendering public policy debate, for promoting positive images of women, and for increasing women's involvement in peace building and the prevention and resolution of conflict.

Figure 3.1 Increasing women's participation in politics (selected countries)

Country	Strategy	Result/outcome
Belize	• Political reform programme launched by the Society for the Promotion of Education and Research. • A Civil Society Summit (1995) in which over 100 organizations participated. • The Belize Organization of Women played a leading role in building alliances among organizations, to strengthen the voice of civil society in the governance of Belize.	• Women's political participation was among the areas identified in the call for political reform. • Development of a People's Manifesto by the Civil Society Movement. • In its Women's Manifesto, the People's United Party committed itself to gender-aware economic policies and to including more women in leadership positions in the public service by appointing women to 30% of the posts.

Country	Strategy	Result/outcome
Jamaica	• Jamaica Women's Caucus formed in 1992 to encourage and facilitate participation of women at the highest levels of active politics and to raise the number of female parliamentarians to 40% of the total number. • The People's National Party developed a strategy to increase the number of women in local government within the context of the local government election in 1998.	• Training programmes to prepare women to run as candidates and to serve as campaign managers. • Establishment of a candidate's fund. • Use of media to increase awareness about the importance of greater participation by women in politics. • Election of a female as well as a male vice-president. • Adoption of a gender equity policy by 700 regional delegates. • Women contested 16 of the 40 divisions in Region 3, the largest electoral region, and won 11 (27.5%) of the seats.
St Kitts—Nevis	• Members at a party convention in 1992 passed a gender parity policy.	• In 1997 women held 3 of the top 5 positions in the party.
Trinidad and Tobago	• Women's organizations formed an alliance and created the Women's Political Platform. • Women candidates from all parties met to discuss the issues. • Used the media to publicize the Platform's Manifesto.	• Post-election meeting of women who had been elected. • Continuing links between female members of parliament and women's organizations. • Women's organizations provide information on issues to politicians.

Source: Adapted from Vassell (1999).

CHAPTER 4

Women's Organizations and the Caribbean Women's Movement

Historically women in the Caribbean have always come together informally in groups to share ideas and experiences, to discuss problems, to explore solutions, to learn from and support each other, and often just to interact and to enjoy each other's company. Such small groups exist in every country even today.

Between 1940 and 1960 several women's organizations had been formed to provide opportunities for women to meet and discuss issues that were of concern to them and to implement programmes to address these issues and to improve women's condition. Among these were the Federation of Women's Institutes, the Women's Corona Society, the Caribbean Women's League, the Mother's Union and the Young Women's Christian Association (YWCA). These organizations were of two types. First, there were welfare organizations – the social clubs, church groups, the YWCA – that did and continue to do a tremendous amount of work to improve women's condition and the quality of life of their families. Their programmes were intended to make women better wives and mothers and included education and training in home-making skills, child care, health and nutrition, and the care of the sick and elderly. Their programmes were not only beneficial to thousands of women but provided a social safety net that supplemented the work of government social welfare departments.

Second, there were organizations that had a political orientation. Among these were the Women's Liberal Club in Jamaica, the League of Women Voters in Trinidad and Tobago, and the Women's Political and Education Organization in Guyana. These organizations were concerned about women's right to the vote and their lack of representation at the highest levels of decision making in their societies. They therefore implemented programmes to educate women about politics and to increase their understanding of political processes. They also agitated for women's rights and in 1952 the League of Women Voters in Trinidad and Tobago pressured government to appoint women to serve as jurors. As a result, other organizations began to be formed, including women's 'arms and wings' of political parties and women's professional associations.

The work of these two types of organizations in the early years of the last century laid the foundation and set the stage for the emergence of a vibrant women's movement in the latter half of the century. They linked the social welfare groups of the 1940s and 1950s to the Women and Development groups of the 1970s and early 1980s and to the activist, feminist groups of the late 1980s and 1990s.

By the 1970s, while many of the women's groups continued in the social welfare tradition, many others began to adopt a developmental approach. Concerned about the high level of unemployment among women, about the low wages that many women received and about their low earning power, they implemented a number of income-generating programmes that attempted to remedy this situation. Many women in poor rural and urban communities participated in and benefited from these programmes. At the same time, a growing concern about abortion and rape and about women's rights to have control over their bodies, stimulated the creation of new organizations like Women Against Rape in Barbados, the Jamaican Association for the Repeal of Abortion Laws, Defence for the Rights of Women in Trinidad and Tobago and Women Against Terrorism in Guyana. The work of these and similar organizations helped to locate women's rights within the larger context of human rights.

In several countries National Councils of Women were also formed. These umbrella organizations focused on increasing awareness of women's condition, on their position of disadvantage *vis-à-vis* that of men in their societies, and on building women's self-esteem and

Box 8 • National Councils/organizations of women

These umbrella organizations are made up of several women's groups of all types and sizes. From the beginning National Councils were faced with many problems and challenges. There was confusion about the role that they were expected to play *vis-à-vis* their member groups, so that instead of taking on a coordinating role many found themselves implementing the same activities and projects as their members. In addition, poor planning and lack of adequate monitoring and evaluation resulted in implementation of large numbers of *ad hoc* and isolated activities and events, and lack of financial and human resources limited what they could undertake and accomplish. This led to many disappointments and failures and to high levels of frustration. The problem of leadership and efficient and effective management also adversely affected their operation.

In spite of these drawbacks, however, these National Councils and their members have played a vital role in providing much-needed services to women and women's groups and in keeping the debate and discussions of women's issues in the public eye. In every country they and their members have implemented and continue to organize public education programmes and campaigns, to host national conferences, seminars and workshops, and to organize education and training programmes in a wide range of subjects and topics for women.

They have also implemented a number of important projects to deal with and address particular problems that women in the region face. Among such projects are the establishment of shelters and halfway houses for battered women, counselling for abused females, scholarship programmes for children, and education, skills training and income-generating programmes for unemployed women.

self-confidence. They also felt that their role was to support, facilitate, coordinate and monitor the activities of their members.

In 1970, five years before the first United Nations Conference on Women, representatives of National Councils and their members met in Guyana to form the first regional organization with a focus on women and women's issues. The launching of CARIWA in 1970 was a milestone in the history of the women's movement in the Caribbean. As a regional body comprised of National Councils and of women's organizations from different countries it provided a forum for women in the region to articulate their concerns and express their views, a platform from which to mobilize women to take collective action to achieve common goals and a mechanism through which they could speak with one voice to make demands of governments.

The Caribbean Women's Association (CARIWA)

CARIWA's objectives were to create and forge linkages among women's organizations in the region, to increase awareness about women's role, position and condition, and to encourage recognition of the contributions of Caribbean women to the development of their societies.

Over the last 30 years CARIWA has held biannual conferences, conducted several training workshops and seminars, and implemented projects for women in several countries. Through its programmes and activities it was instrumental in bringing women to the forefront and getting them appointed to prominent positions. It lobbied for and succeeded in getting CARICOM to establish a Women's Desk within the secretariat and was one of the organizations responsible for the creation of the Women and Development Unit at the University of the West Indies.

As an NGO, however, like its members and other women's groups, it has experienced many constraints and faced many challenges. The Association is run entirely on a voluntary basis and has not been able to acquire the financial support necessary to establish a secretariat or to implement the numerous and varied programmes and projects that it would like. In spite of this, it has survived because of the commitment and dedication of the women who have been its leaders over the years. Moreover, it has had an impact not only on the lives of many women but on national leaders and decision makers, and consequently on policies that address women's issues.

The Women and Development Unit (WAND), UWI

The Women and Development Unit was created in 1978 by women attending a regional conference on Women in Development in the Caribbean. These women saw the need for a regional organization with the status, credibility and clout to speak to and for women, to advocate on their behalf and to advance the debate for their advancement at the national, regional and international levels. From the beginning, therefore, WAND was seen as being different from other existing women's organizations.

Its location within the university and especially within the outreach arm, the Extra-Mural Department, gave it the flexibility to work with women at all levels of the society that it would not have had if placed within an academic faculty. It also provided it with the opportunity to reach a wider constituency and to define and create a different relationship between the university and its constituency, and between academia and activism. At the same time it gained access to a wider range of resources than other women's organizations.

Recognizing the important role that women's organizations had to play within its programmes, WAND paid a great deal of attention to strengthening and building the capacity of National Councils and their member groups. At the same time it worked with and lobbied governments to establish National Machineries for the Advancement of Women in each country and within the CARICOM secretariat itself. In this way it helped governments and NGOs, as well as national and regional organizations, to understand that they all had different but complementary roles to play in changing and improving the situation of women.

The WAND approach
WAND's programmes included consciousness raising and awareness building, networking and advocacy, capacity building through technical assistance and training, and pilot projects to explore and experiment with alternative approaches to development. It adopted a participatory methodology that put the reality and experience of women at the core

of its work. By so doing it highlighted the valuable contribution that women were making to their countries and legitimized their claims for greater recognition, more opportunities and increased benefits from national development programmes and projects.

Through the many programmes and projects implemented in several communities throughout the region WAND has touched the lives of thousands of women and many men. Through its training programmes many individuals, including field workers in several countries, acquired skills in the use of the participatory methodology and now use these in their practice. WAND is also well known for its pilot projects, the most famous of which is the Rose Hall project in St Vincent, started in 1981 and continuing even today. Within these projects WAND worked with NGOs and CBOs in several rural communities in several countries to experiment with alternative development models and strategies.

WAND in the 1990s

One outcome of these experiments was a gradual shift from the concept of integrating women into development, to empowering women. By 1995, influenced by the involvement of the coordinator in the Third World women's organization Development Alternatives with Women for a New Era (DAWN), WAND had become more political and feminist in its orientation. Consequently the focus of its programmes shifted from integrating women into development, and from an approach based on providing technical assistance to support gradual change, to one committed to the empowerment of women and to the implementation of programmes designed to encourage and facilitate social change together with the transformation of women's lives and of their communities.

WAND's work in the region has been a comprehensive programme aimed at developing men and women in communities, raising their awareness about women's issues, increasing their competence and capacity to direct and manage their own development and to take control of their lives, and thus helping them to participate actively in the development of their communities.

The UN World conference on Women in 1975 and the emergence of a strong international women's movement introduced new perspectives and led to a shift in focus and emphasis in the work of women's organizations in the region. It caused existing organizations to rethink their roles and to implement new programmes, and it led to the creation of new and different types of organizations.

Following the recommendations of the World Conference many of the organizations turned their attention to Women in Development (WID) issues and began to implement programmes and projects aimed at 'integrating women into development'. As a result they were able to highlight women's role in and contribution to national and regional development, and to examine more closely the relationship between women's roles and the process and outcomes of development initiatives. In doing so they became more aware that women were already making significant and important contributions to the development of their countries and that they had been doing so since the days of slavery. Moreover, in discussing and debating this issue, it became clear that women had not always benefited from development policies, plans and programmes commensurately with the level of their contributions.

One of the organizations that implemented several WID projects was the Women and Development Unit (WAND) of the UWI. The important and significant contribution made by WAND to the advancement of Caribbean women is well known and recognized not only in the region but also internationally. WAND stands out as a model of what can be achieved with the 'right' philosophy and with innovative approaches, commitment and dedication. Through its work WAND has made a significant and important contribution to the development of women, people and societies in the Caribbean, and to the women's movement in the Caribbean and internationally. The 'WAND Approach' has been widely used by women's groups and organizations; it has been studied by many universities around the world and endorsed by international agencies involved with women. It has been recognized and used as an important strategy for creating critical political consciousness in women as well as in decision making, for linking micro problems to macro issues and national policies, and for addressing gender issues in non-threatening ways. WAND's success can be traced to the vision of its coordinator, to her commitment and dedication to the cause of women, and to the enthusiasm of the women who have worked with and in it over the years, and to their belief that their work could and was making a difference.

By the mid-1980s, while many organizations continued in the welfare tradition and many continued to focus on women's role in development and on meeting their practical needs, several also began to implement programmes designed to address their strategic needs. The focus of their programmes was not only on improving women's condition, but emphasized the importance of removing barriers and obstacles that prevented them from achieving their full potential and from being awarded an equal place alongside men in their societies. Advocacy and lobbying therefore became important dimensions of their work and, in addition to focusing on issues like the high rate of unemployment among women and the low wages often paid to them, they stressed the importance of equal pay for equal work. Their concern about women's rights and their lack of representation in politics, their awareness of gender discrimination and their agitation against it all reflected a feminist orientation, even though the word had not yet become familiar to many in the region.

At this time, too, a number of feminist activist groups began to emerge. Their programmes were intended to help women gain a deeper understanding of the societal factors and structures, arrangements and procedures that contribute to, reinforce and perpetuate oppression of and discrimination against women, and to transform women's reality. Influenced by DAWN and by a feminist analysis that critically examined structural inequalities, these groups introduced yet another dimension and perspective into the work of women's organizations.

WAND was instrumental in the formation of some of these 'new' organizations, including the Women and Development Studies Groups on the three campuses of UWI, and CAFRA. Their creation ushered in a new phase in the history of women's organizations and of the women's movement in the region. Because of their feminist

The Caribbean Association for Feminist Research and Action (CAFRA)

CAFRA was launched in Barbados in 1985 at the end of an all-day meeting facilitated by WAND and attended by 40 women, feminists and activists. It is a network of feminists from all language groups in the Caribbean region.

Its mission is to channel the collective power of women for individual and societal transformation. CAFRA recognizes that there is a relationship between women's oppression and other types of oppression in the society: through its work it attempts to address this and to influence policy to eradicate oppression and to promote and ensure gender equity and equality. CAFRA has a feminist political agenda. Its work is grounded in feminist ideology and informed by an analysis that seeks to understand the social relations of gender and the factors that contribute to gender inequalities and gender discrimination.

Its main activities are research, advocacy, training, documentation and information sharing, and it has implemented several projects in each of these areas. Among these have been research projects on women in agriculture, on the impact of new trade agreements on rural women, on domestic violence, on women and the law, on gender and human rights, on women's health and reproductive rights, and on gender and trade. It has also organized conferences and seminars on women in politics, feminist theory, women's history and creative expression, among others. Its Summer Institute in Feminist Theory for Women Activists (1992) exposed participants to a wide range of topics that increased their understanding of the historical context and theoretical framework within which the women's movement, feminism and women's studies has emerged, developed and grown.

CAFRA publishes a magazine, *CAFRA News*, and produces and disseminates a number of papers and articles that document the findings of its research, and that provide information about the outcomes of its various activities. Based on the in-depth political analysis undertaken, its articles and documents provide insights and contribute to a deeper understanding of the structural factors and societal mechanisms that contribute to and perpetuate gender inequalities.

The scope, breadth and depth of CAFRA's work has ushered in a new phase in the women's struggle and of women organizing for social change and gender equity and equality, and is contributing in significant ways to the growth of a feminist movement in the region.

orientation and the approaches and strategies that they use they were significantly different from their counterparts of the previous decades. CAFRA's work has been impressive. The organization has not only brought a different dimension to women's struggle for equality, but through its various programmes and activities it has touched and made a difference to many women's lives.

> As a woman CAFRA has taught me to learn more about women, that now it is time to stand up for our rights, learn to be independent, earn our own money and live your life how you want to.

> It is within CAFRA that we first saw possibilities and dreamed dreams of joining the march for gender equality.

Another important event in the development of women's organizations was the creation of Women in Development Studies Groups on the UWI campuses in Jamaica, Trinidad and Barbados, and at the University of Guyana (UG). Building on the work of WAND, these groups of women in the universities brought an academic perspective to the work on women and women's issues. They organized seminars, produced academic papers and articles, engaged in research, and began to incorporate women's issues into their teaching and academic discourses.

In 1987, these groups, with support from the Institute of Social Studies in The Hague, implemented a project on Teaching and Research in Women and Development Studies, within which interdisciplinary seminars were a major activity. These seminars, in addition to sensitizing the university community to women and gender issues, provided a forum for faculty members to explore these

The Centre for Gender and Development Studies, UWI

An outgrowth of the pioneering work done by WAND and by the Development Studies Groups, the Centre's programmes focus on research, teaching and outreach. Its aim is to introduce and maintain an interdisciplinary programme of gender and development studies and to encourage and facilitate integration of gender issues in all disciplines within the university, through research to generate data on women and gender issues, and to develop linkages and relationships with institutions and organizations concerned about and working on these issues.

The Centre promotes, facilitates and conducts interdisciplinary research on women and on gender. Among its research topics have been projects on gender and the economy, the construction of Caribbean masculinities and the impact of Christian teaching on women's sexuality. The Centre also offers undergraduate courses in areas such as Gender in Caribbean Culture and Gender Issues in Agriculture, while at the graduate level it offers a Master of Science, Master of Philosophy and Doctor of Philosophy in Gender and Development Studies.

Since 1994 the Centre on the Cave Hill campus has offered a biennial certificate course in Gender and Development Studies as part of its outreach programme. One of the objectives of this course is to strengthen academic teaching and to reach out to women and men in the non-campus territories of the Windward Islands. In this regard it has also organized workshops for the resident tutors in the university centres of the non-campus territories to increase their awareness of the importance of including gender and gender perspectives into their programmes.

Conferences, public lectures, seminars and workshops are also a regular feature of the Centre's programme on each of the campuses, and these are often carried out in collaboration with national and regional agencies. Participants include government officials, representatives of local and regional institutions and agencies, representatives of women's groups and organizations, and secondary school students. Topics covered in these activities have included Gender in Public Policy and Planning, Gender and Counselling in Sexual and Reproductive Health, the Construction of Caribbean Masculinities, Gender and Self-Esteem, Women in Literature, and Women in Politics.

The Centre has also produced an impressive number of publications and has contributed to an understanding of feminist theory and the development of feminist scholarship in the Caribbean.

issues in some depth. They also laid the groundwork for the integration of women's issues, and gender issues in their various disciplines. The papers presented and discussed at these seminars provided the basis for courses in women, gender and development issues that were subsequently incorporated into the curricula of several disciplines.

As a result of these activities, UWI eventually established the Centre for Gender and Development Studies, which has had a tremendous impact in the region. Not only has it been responsible for putting gender onto the university's curriculum, but it has also increased awareness of the importance of understanding gender as a social construct and an analytical tool, while equipping a number of women and men with the skills in gender analysis and gender planning needed to analyse social and economic phenomena from a gender perspective and to develop gender-sensitive policies and programmes.

The Caribbean women's movement

The concept of a movement involves the idea of a large mass of people organizing themselves and mobilizing others to agitate and work towards a goal of righting wrongs that affect them as a group. While there is agreement about the existence of a large number and wide variety of women's organizations and widespread recognition of their accomplishments and of the valuable work that they do, there are still those who question whether there is or ever has been a women's movement in the Caribbean. For them, while women work in their own organizations, large numbers of these organizations continue to work in isolation and often in competition with each other. Moreover, they argue that much of the work of women's organizations responds to existing demands, and that their programmes are geared to meet the specific needs of their members rather than to address the issues facing all women. Recent research carried out with members of the National Organization of Women in Barbados produced evidence that supports this view. Another view is that while elements of a women's movement have been visible in countries like Jamaica, Grenada and St Vincent, its development has been uneven and it is questionable whether it ever existed in others like Barbados. At the same time it has been pointed out that while there are now a number of feminist groups, they have no mass base and have not been able to mobilize large numbers of ordinary women nor women's organizations. Large numbers of women cannot and do not relate to the feminist organizations, regarding them as being either too intellectual or too removed from their experience and too insensitive to their reality.

Like all other socialist movements the Caribbean women's movement has been influenced by the particular cultural, political, economic and social context out of which it emerged and within which it operated. At the same time it has also been influenced by international events and trends and by their impact on the lives of Caribbean women. In the 1970s the Caribbean women's movement was influenced by other social movements including the Black Power movement and the international women's movement. Discussions with some women revealed that, for some, the former had a greater impact on their lives than did the latter.

I gained more from the Black Power movement. I gained a sense of identity and of who I am, and I felt proud and not ashamed to be a black woman.

At the same time some women's organizations aligned themselves to or were part of left-wing political parties like the New Jewel movement in Grenada, and like them began to agitate for broad-based social change and, within this context, for change in women's status, position and condition.

The movement in the 1970s was vibrant and dynamic, debate on women's issues intense, and the amount of activity tremendous. Fuelled by the enthusiasm and commitment of women and supported by resources from the international community, women's organizations were able to mobilize thousands of women in communities across the region to work for their own improvement. They organized public education programmes and rallies, and their conferences, seminars and workshops, which focused on various aspects of women's lives, became a regular feature. They created an environment in which women from every level of Caribbean society were made to feel confident, motivated to speak out and share their experiences and their hopes for a better future. National and regional conferences organized by women's organizations also provided opportunities for women to interact with government officials and for the latter to listen to women, to hear their concerns; they provided a platform for women to make demands for changes in national policies that created barriers and obstacles to women's advancement.

In the 1970s the women's movement created togetherness among women and gave them a new awareness.

'I didn't know that other women were experiencing the same pain until I went to a women's meeting. I saw that women shared the same disadvantage.

The movement instilled a sense of identity.

Women came out in solidarity for a cause.

During the 1970s and into the mid 1980s there was a significant increase in the number of women's groups and organizations consciously working to address women's issues, to transform social and gender relations, and to bring about fundamental change in societal institutions. The movement reflected the rich diversity of the Caribbean population and women of all colours, classes and political ideologies, were actively advocating for change, for the advancement of women and for women's rights. They brought a wide variety of ideas, styles and approaches, and developed and used networking as a strategy and a tool for engaging NGOs, government and the universities in the struggle for gender equity and equality. The high level of mass activity and activism during this period also led women and women's organizations to confront governments and to demand changes in laws and policies that would end oppression and discrimination against women. Their demands resulted in legal reforms, in some new legislation and in women's issues being put on the national agenda.

However, some women were of the view that the movement was being used by governments that were mouthing the rhetoric of women's development and women's rights but were not really committed to providing the resources needed to achieve these goals.

Government used the women's movement to get resources to do what they wanted, but these resource were not always necessarily used to or for women's benefit.

The result was a great deal of frustration and disillusionment among women and this in turn could have been responsible for a 'slowing down' in the momentum and pace of the movement. While the movement seemed to have lost some of its dynamism, however, this period saw the emergence of more activist and feminist groups whose concern was to increase women's understanding of the factors that contribute to, reinforce and perpetuate gender oppression and discrimination.

In the late 1980s the women's movement appeared to become fragmented and dispersed and it became more difficult to mobilize women to agitate for change. In spite of this, and in response to the need to continue to increase awareness of women's disadvantaged position *vis-à-vis* their male counterparts, women's organizations embarked on a number of programmes that focused on the economic, social and political factors that were contributing to gender inequalities. Many more organizations also implemented public education programmes and began to use popular education techniques to raise awareness of and to initiate discussion on the structural inequalities that exist in society.

The emergence of organizations like CAFRA and the Centre for Gender and Development Studies at the University of the West Indies not only influenced women's organizations and their approach to the struggle for equality and equal rights for women, but heralded a new phase in the history of the Caribbean women's movement. Their use of activities like research and intellectual discourse moved the debate on women's concerns to a new level and introduced an intellectual dimension into the movement that had not been there before. They created linkages and actively collaborated with international agencies and with women's organizations in other parts of the world, and so moved the Caribbean women's agenda into the international arena, locating the Caribbean women's movement within the international women's movement.

During the last decade of the last century, the women's movement appeared again to be gathering momentum. One indicator of this is the way that women's organizations in the region mobilized women and themselves to participate in the Fourth World Conference on Women in Beijing in 1995. On the initiative and with the support of UNIFEM's area office, and in collaboration with CARICOM and other regional bodies, women's groups came together and developed a strategy that linked the work of women's organizations, researchers and activists to government's preparations for the conference. Representatives of women's organizations in and from all countries collectively reviewed their experiences over the previous decades, analysing them within the context of global and international trends. They agreed on their major concerns and priority issues and presented these in a 'Platform Document' prepared by CAFRA.

Because of their combined efforts, their preparation and the strategy they adopted, many of the positions on which they had agreed were reflected in the final conference document. As a result of the well-structured preparatory work undertaken by the women's organizations, several women were involved in the preparatory conferences, over five hundred Caribbean women participated and were actively involved in discussions, and several played leading roles in the Conference. They chaired committees on health, on poverty and on women's work, they facilitated consensus on controversial issues, provided leadership to some delegations, and sat on a panel of eminent persons.

During the last decade of the last century, the women's movement again appears to be gathering momentum as organizations turn their attention to some of the critical issues facing women at the beginning of the new millennium. Among these are globalization, poverty, abuse and violence against women, power sharing, and a shift of attention to gender and the role of 'men's issues'. It also appears that the shift in focus to gender is resulting in a move to downplay the feminist political agenda. One of the challenges facing women's organizations is therefore to address the issue of the place of feminism within the movement. As women seek to deal with these issues, women's organizations are continuing their role of providing women with relevant and up-to-date information, are developing strategies to address women's concerns and meet their needs, and are establishing structures to support women as they struggle to come to terms with the challenges confronting them in the new millennium.

The shift in focus from women's issues to gender has also led to a growing concern among women and women's organizations that this shift could derail the women's movement to such an extent that it will not be able to achieve its goals.

> *Change is blowing the movement away from a focus on women into the direction of gender.*

> *We must be careful that the gender agenda does not relegate the women's movement to a state where it is always learning and not reaching the point of changing the situation and the statistics.*

The growth of feminism

The history of feminism in the Caribbean began with slave women's resistance and with the women's movement in the early years of the last century. In the 1980s this was influenced by the emergence of a network of Third World feminists and the creation of DAWN. Their analytical input provided the women's movement worldwide with tools for advancing a different perspective on women in development issues, and for increasing their understanding of the links between micro-level community work and the macro-economic frameworks within which women operate and that impact on their lives.

In 1992 WAND and CAFRA organized the Summer Institute in Feminist Theory. Over a period of two weeks, 28 women from communities across the region were exposed to eight modules that introduced then to a feminist perspective on the day-to-day experiences of women, and on social issues that were areas of concern not only to feminists but also to all Caribbean women. Through a process of reflection and analysis of individual and collective experiences, participants were conscientized and became more aware of the importance of informing themselves of the factors that impact on their lives, of the outcomes, and of the need to take responsibility for and control of their lives.

> One of the most important things that came out to me is that as a woman you have to know what is going on around you and take responsibility for your own life.

Within the academic context of UWI, the work of the Centre for Gender and Development Studies is encouraging and facilitating the development and greater understanding of feminist theory and of feminism. At the level of the community, however, there is still a great deal of resistance to feminism and suspicion of feminists. For large numbers of women in the region, these terms have a negative connotation linked to man hating and bra burning, and for this reason many women don't want to be associated with feminism or to be called feminists. This is so even among women who are committed to and are working to improve women's condition and to address women's concerns.

There is a feeling among some that feminists have ignored the history of women's groups and negated the struggles of the women's movement, that feminism has no mass base and that it has alienated many women including young women. Generally speaking, young women have not identified with and have not been actively involved in the women's movement or become activists.

Given that over half of the population in most Caribbean countries is under 30 years of age, one of the failures of the feminist movement is its inability to attract and maintain the interest of young women and the almost complete exclusion of females under the age of 18 years. This exclusion of large numbers of women means that the views and opinions as well as the needs and concerns of most Caribbean women are not represented by existing feminist organizations (Goddard 1995).

The inclusion of young sisters is crucial.

Moreover, many young women in the region say:

We don't know what the struggle is all about. You (older women), say that you had a struggle and were trying to bring us to a point, but we don't understand the struggle that you older women are talking about.

In the 1970s and 1980s women set a foundation for the struggle and a momentum and pace for the women's movement, but young women in the 1990s and at the beginning of the new millennium appear not to be able to relate to this and feel alienated from the activities of the last two decades. They see themselves differently; they see men differently; their struggle is different and the issues they face are different from those of their mothers. As one young woman remarked:

You fought for the right to get certain jobs; we have the jobs, but our problem is what is happening to us on the job and how to deal with it.

Young professional women find themselves in positions and situations in which they are faced with contradictions and conflicts as they struggle to define and negotiate their personal and professional relationships with men. But the women's movement and recent gender training programmes have not yet adequately addresses these issues nor, according to those at whom they are directed, have they helped young

Caribbean women to negotiate and deal with their main concerns successfully.

On one hand, largely as a result of the women's movement, some young women have become more vocal and outspoken in their relationships with men and are no longer willing to 'take crap from men'. On the other hand, some in the society, including some women, see this trend towards more 'aggressive' behaviour as having negative effects and young women are being accused and chastised for flaunting their bodies, exploiting men for sex and money, and for being interested in a series of short-term relationships with different men rather than in a long-term relationship with a single partner. In addition there is a feeling and some evidence to suggest that young women, as well as young men, now expect and accept that violence will be a part of male–female relationships.

These issues have not yet been taken up in any serious way by women's organizations in the region. This failure of the movement to embrace the younger generation and to address their particular issues and concerns has implications, not only for the movement's future, but also for future generations of women.

At the First Caribbean Feminist Encounter held in Trinidad in December 1998, participants identified some of the challenges that are facing the women's movement in the Caribbean. Among these are:

- the need to strengthen existing organizations;

- the need for strategies to transfer ideas and information from one generation of women to the next, and the need to create new organizations with and for each new generation of women;

- the perception of many young women that feminism is either irrelevant or dead;

- the need to develop strategies to handle difference and diversity among women;

- the backlash in which women are being blamed for the 'marginalization of Caribbean men';

- the creation and maintenance of feminist models of democracy within women's organizations;

- the development of more creative strategies to articulate the direction of a women's movement and of a feminist movement in the Caribbean.

While many questions surround the existence, nature and type of a feminist movement in the region, it is important to recognize the difference between the women's movement and the evolving feminist movement, to acknowledge the different contributions that each is making to the ongoing debate on women's issues and gender issues, and the ways in which their work is leading to and resulting in societal changes to bring about more equitable and just societies.

∽

There can be no doubt that women's organizations in the Caribbean have had many impressive achievements, and that there is a women's movement in the Caribbean. Women's organizations have played a critical role in placing women's issues and gender on the development agenda of Caribbean countries. They have played an important role in advocating for women's rights, and in lobbying for policies and laws that take women's concerns and needs into consideration and that seek to end gender oppression and discrimination. They have highlighted and drawn attention to women's activities and the vital contributions that women are making to the development of their countries and of the region as a whole. They have built and developed links and relationships with government and with other civil society organizations and agencies.

However, some feminists and feminist organizations believe too many women's organizations are lacking in feminist leadership, that too few have undertaken a critical, political analysis of women's oppression and discrimination, and that they therefore have not fully understood the deep and far-reaching effects that gender inequalities and gender inequity can have on women, on men and on the society as a whole.

There also seems to be some justification for the accusation and for the concern that some of the existing organizations, as well as the Caribbean women's movement itself, has excluded and continues to exclude some groups of (especially younger) women and to ignore their particular concerns.

These are but some of the many challenges that Caribbean women, women's organizations and the Caribbean women's movement are facing in the new millennium.

CHAPTER 5

Mechanisms and Strategies for the Advancement and Empowerment of Women

Mechanisms for the advancement of women evolved out of women's struggle for equality and out of the focus on women's position of disadvantage, highlighted by the UN international conferences. In the Caribbean during the last quarter of the twentieth century governments as well as NGOs employed several mechanisms and adopted a variety of strategies to promote and facilitate women's advancement.

National Machineries for the Advancement of Women

During the 1970s and 1980s several countries established national commissions on the status of women and, based on their reports, developed national policies on women. Every country also established a National Machinery for the Advancement of Women. Initially these were Women's Bureaux and Women's Desks, but later some governments created Divisions, Departments and even Ministries of Women's Affairs. Between 1974 and 1976 Women's Bureaux were established in four countries. The first was established in Jamaica, followed by Antigua, Barbados and Grenada. During the 1980s Women's Desks were established in most of the independent countries and in the 1990s in the Dependent Overseas Territories.

In 1983 the Commonwealth secretariat carried out a study on National Machineries in the region and found that their objectives were not clear, that they had been given responsibility but little authority, that they lacked the human and financial resources needed to be effective, and that although they had some field staff, few had the professional staff needed to do research, policy analysis and impact studies, or to produce reports and articles on a regular basis. Furthermore, discussions with government officials revealed that there was a lack of understanding about the role and function of National Machinery. Between 1983 and 1985 some attempts were made by governments to upgrade the status of the Machineries and to provide them with more resources, but in almost all cases they continued to suffer from uncertainty about their role and function as well as from a lack of adequate human and financial resources.[1] In many cases only very small allocations were made to the Machineries from national budgets and they were forced to depend on funding from international agencies. By the mid-1990s, although many governments had issued national policy statements on women, and although these had been approved by the various cabinets, Machineries were faced with serious challenges as they attempted to translate these statements into goals and objectives.

At the regional level, in 1981 the CARICOM secretariat appointed a Women's Affairs Officer and later established a Women's Desk. This played a major role in the development and strengthening of the National Machineries, providing advice to governments and technical assistance, identifying and channelling financial resources, recruiting experts and consultants, organizing training for staff and commissioning and supporting research. In the 1980s the secretariat organized the first meeting of Ministers with Responsibility for Women's Affairs, and these are now a regular event along with meetings of other ministers of government. Through its work the CARICOM Women's Desk has been responsible for putting women's affairs and gender on the political agenda of the secretariat.

Two strategies that have been used by National Machineries in several countries in their attempts to influence sectoral policies and programmes are the creation of inter-ministerial committees and 'Focal Points' in key ministries. The committees and Focal Points are intended to inform the Machineries of the plans and programmes of their ministries and departments, and to explore and agree on strategies for incorporating women's issues and a gender perspective into them. In several cases, however, the individuals appointed to represent their ministries are women, who are usually not in key positions and who are limited in their power and ability to influence policy. As a result while some of these committees meet regularly and have been able to achieve some of their objectives, and while some of the Focal Points do make efforts to include women's concerns and gender issues into their programmes, they have not been as effective as was originally expected. Consequently, in some countries women' issues and gender are still treated as a separate topic and not as an integral part of the work of every government ministry and department.

These shortcomings were discussed at the seventh meeting of CARICOM Ministers with Responsibility for Women's Affairs, held in the Bahamas in 1995. Here participants recognized that, in spite of national policy statements and several workshops to strengthen them, National Machineries had not been given the type and level of authority required to influence national policies or to initiate the widespread societal changes needed to achieve gender equity. There is therefore probably some justification to the belief that governments were and still are not really committed to dealing with women's concerns and gender issues, and only pay lip service and spout the rhetoric because it is politic so to do.

The placement of National Machinery in 'soft' ministries like community development rather than in ministries of finance and planning has contributed to their low status and to the general lack of respect accorded them by government officials. This, coupled with a lack of resources, has severely limited their work and minimized their impact on the national agenda. As a result, while all of the Machineries have been able to implement, with some success, a significant number of Women in Development programmes and several micro-level projects to meet some of women's practical needs for increased income, better housing, education and training, and although they have also implemented several consciousness-raising and awareness-building programmes for women, few have succeeded in influencing national or sectoral policies addressed to women's strategic needs.

In spite of the limitations of the National Machineries and the constraints faced by their directors, over the last two decades, mainly with technical assistance and support from regional and international agencies, they have implemented a large number and a wide variety of education and training programmes, projects and activities at the community level, and through these have been able to make a difference in the lives of thousands of women throughout the region. For example the Department of Gender Affairs in Trinidad and Tobago implemented a project aimed at economic empowerment of community businesswomen, and the same department in Grenada has implemented a number of projects for women in rural communities.

Nationally sponsored consciousness raising, public education and advocacy programmes have kept debates on women's issues and gender alive. For example, the Gender Affairs Department in St Lucia, as part of a national project on gender-based violence, implemented a public education and media programme on the subject, and the Department in Trinidad organized a national conference on Women in Leadership. All of the Machineries have organized national conferences on women and more recently on gender, and their reports and position papers have been critical in shaping the agendas of the biennial conferences of Ministers with Responsibility for Women's Affairs.

While the National Machineries have achieved much with few resources, and while in theory governments in the region have acknowledged their importance, it also appears that policy makers and senior government officials are still not clear about the role and function of the Machineries. This is reflected in the fact that in many countries they are still located in what are regarded as the 'soft ministries', that they are still understaffed and under-resourced, and that some governments have changed their names to include 'Gender' without apparently having given serious thought to the implications for national policy and programmes of this move. In many countries the name change has been the only change to date. While there is an urgent need to reassess the role and function of National Machineries, it is important to ensure that in doing so the focus on women's problems, concerns and issues is not jeopardized or minimized.

In 1999, in order to find out what women and men in St Kitts expected from the Women's Affairs Department in the new millennium, the Department randomly sought opinions from a number of individuals. Their responses reflect not only their expectations, but also opinions about the role, function and performance of the Department. A brief examination of a sample of the responses, quoted below, reveals some differences between the types of response received from women and those received from men.

It appears that women were interested in and impressed by programmes that were intended to improve women's position, that addressed women's issues, and from which women did and would benefit. On the other hand, the responses from men seemed to be concerned more about the shift to gender and the need to clarify the Department's position on this in relation to women's issues. Male responses also appear to highlight the need for clear policies.

Responses from both men and women reveal a recognition that the programmes of the Women's Affairs Department have increased awareness of women's issues, that they had some positive impact on women's lives and that they should be continued. However, the responses also suggest that the Department needs to pay more attention to policy, to be more focused in its programming, and to clarify its role and function in relation to women's issues and gender issues.

Responses from women

Continue to implement awareness programmes in your usual creative way.

Concentrate on the total development of women, not just on physical abuse.

Continue skills training programmes to help encourage employment.

Do more empowerment work, follow-up programmes with teen mothers and be more concerned with media watch.

Address the disparity in salary between males and females, make it more equitable.

Help women to gain more access to credit.

Continue the training in the gender management system.

Responses from men

Have a clear orientation, Gender vs Women's Affairs.

You have really done a good job with your awareness programmes so far, now you need to have the goods to deliver and you need to work on attitudes.

Stop focusing on women and focus on gender.

Create programmes to sensitize men about the changing roles in society.

Empower women to run the country and concentrate on our local problems. North American women's problems are not the same as our local women's problems.

Go out into schools and help develop esteem programmes for our boys, since they have no role models.

You need to prioritize instead of focusing on everything.

You need to have more clear-cut policies and to be more aggressive in your approach.

With the increased attention being paid to gender issues, in recent years governments in some countries – for example Antigua and Barbuda, Barbados, St Lucia, and Trinidad and Tobago – have changed the names of their National Machineries to Departments or Divisions of Gender Affairs. On the whole, this name change appears to have occurred without any clear understanding of the reason for the change; of the difference in role, function and programming; or of the implication and impact of the change on women and on men. So far, only in Trinidad and Tobago has the Department of Gender Affairs articulated a new goal and developed specific strategies to reflect the name change and the shift in direction. The goal is to mainstream gender in all policies, plans and programmes, and the strategies that will be adopted to achieve this include the creation of a gender policy, legislative reform in support of gender equity, and extensive gender training at all levels.

In some of the other countries, however, such decisive steps have not yet been taken and the staff of these 'new' departments, for example in St Lucia and in Barbados, although they are continuing their work and may also have begun to pay more attention to gender issues, are still not sure about the status of the department or of the expectations of government or of the public. In Barbados this is particularly notice-able: over the last few years the Department's public profile has been very low-key and there is little information available on its programmes.

Legal reform

Over the last 25 years every country in the Caribbean has engaged in legislative reform and has introduced new legislation to improve the status of women and to ensure that their rights are not violated and that they are not discriminated against because of their sex. Many of the legal reforms resulted from commissions on the status of women set up by governments in the 1970s. In 1972, at its seventh conference of heads of governments, CARICOM was asked to 'recommend leg-islative action designed to remove constitutional and other forms of discrimination against women' (CARICOM and ILO 1995: 4). Since then all Caribbean countries have signed the Convention on the Elimination of All Forms of Discrimination Against Women (CEDAW).

To date the CARICOM secretariat has drafted model legislation on citizenship, sexual offences, sexual harassment, domestic violence, equal pay, inheritance, maintenance, and equal opportunity and treat-ment in employment. The secretariat has also printed booklets explaining the model legislation and has conducted workshops in several countries on the different models for members of the judicial services, for women and for the general public.

In every country, too, new legislation has been enacted on such issues as maternity rights, equal pay and child maintenance; in some countries, family laws have been revised and reformed.

Research

Another strategy that has been used to advance and empower women is research. As individuals, groups and organizations in the region participated in international conferences and meetings, and as they became more aware of women's position of disadvantage *vis-à-vis* that of men, they recognized the need to examine the situation of Caribbean women more closely, collecting information that would provide them with a more accurate picture of their status and condition. Thus they began to build and expand the database on Caribbean women.

In doing so they recognized the need for research that focused on women, and was carried out, analysed and interpreted by women themselves; and for the research findings to be used by women as the basis for action to improve their situation and condition. As a result, during the late 1970s and early 1980s a number of researchers and women working in the field of Women in Development became involved in activities that ranged from macro research studies, conducted at the regional level in practically all of the countries, to micro studies conducted in separate communities in several countries. In the process they experimented with different research approaches and methodologies and used data collection methods and techniques to collect qualitative data: the aim was always to obtain more accurate and concrete information from women about their position and condition, their reality and experience, and their actual rather than their stereotypic roles.

Early in the 1980s the Institute of Social and Economic Research at the Cave Hill campus of the UWI implemented the Women in the Caribbean Project (WICP), involving region-wide research carried out in several countries. One of its outputs was a number of research papers with concrete data on various aspects of women's lives, their perceptions and experiences: with the law, in the family, in politics, in education, in work and in agriculture.

The implementation and completion of this research project created the momentum for a long period of research activity on the lives and experiences of Caribbean women. Since then several research studies have been carried out at the regional, national and community levels by academics and researchers from universities, by women's organizations and by women in poor rural communities.

In some countries, like Grenada, national surveys on women have been carried out. Some have produced baseline data; others have identified women's involvement in and contribution to different sectors of the economy. Among these have been surveys and studies in Dominica, St Lucia and St Vincent on women's role in agriculture, while in Trinidad there have been studies on the high use of pesticides, with its impact on women's health, and on the role of professional women in agriculture. Within the last few years research has been done on the impact of the restructuring of the banana industry on women in the Windward Islands, and on the impact of new trade agreements on women in rural communities in the region. In Barbados and in St Lucia studies have been done on women in manufacturing and in industry, and in Jamaica on female participation and performance in education. Several studies have also been done on female unemployment and on women's health, and a few on female participation in politics and decision making. More recently there has been an increase in the amount of research being carried out on violence against women and, within the last five years, on women, gender and poverty.

At the micro level, studies have been carried out in communities in several islands on women's role in the family, household, community and workplace. Within these community-based research studies, a participatory research approach has been used to involve women actively in all phases of the research process, from problem identification to the interpretation and use of research data as the basis for collective action to bring about change. This has been the case in the Rose Hall pilot project on the Integration of Women in Rural Development in St Vincent (since 1981), the Integrated Rural Development Project implemented in three communities in St Lucia

THE ADVANCEMENT AND EMPOWERMENT OF WOMEN · 101

(1983–6), and the regional CORE project implemented in 13 communities in seven countries. In all cases women were actively involved in a process that involved investigating of their communities and examining their lives. This they did by undertaking community surveys, collection of baseline data, problem identification and needs assessment. They also collected data on specific issues related to women such as their use of energy and fuel, high unemployment, health and male–female relations.

Together these macro and micro research studies have produced a large amount of concrete quantitative and qualitative data, and the process of systematic collection and recording has created a large and growing database on Caribbean women. It has also yielded a greater insight and understanding of women's experiences from their perspective, and a recognition of the factors that contribute to their positional disadvantage.

Individual women as well as groups of women have benefited tremendously from being actively involved in research activities. Not only have their knowledge and skills increased and their horizons broadened, but they have also become empowered and been motivated to achieve more for themselves. Evidence of this can be seen in the following statements by local women who coordinated and were involved in the research project on Women in Caribbean Agriculture carried out by CAFRA in Dominica and St Vincent in 1987–8.

> It has opened doors of opportunities, contributed to my own growth and development, given my life added purpose, and has been an impetus for educational achievement.

> Our training as researchers has enabled us to bring a new dimension to our work and enabled us to bring a gender analysis to bear on assumptions that inform social development.

Another outcome of research studies at national and community level is the recognition that women and men participate in and benefit from development programmes and activities in different ways, and that national policies impact on them differently. As a result in the last decade more emphasis has been given to policy research and policy analysis. This type of research is seen as being essential in order to examine national policies and programmes and to assess with a greater degree of accuracy the different ways in which they impact on men and women, and the extent of that difference. In some countries workshops have been held to provide opportunities for policy makers and programme planners to analyse sectoral policies from a gender perspective. A recent workshop for women's organizations in one country identified and analysed the impact of recent economic policies on women in the informal sector; as a result, participants were able to understand how globalization has led their government to formulate economic policies that are having a negative impact on women.

As a result there is now a growing recognition of the need to disaggregate data by sex and gender so as to provide more accurate information on and understanding of where women are placed in the society and of what they do, and to gain a better understanding about their problems and concerns. To address the issue of sex-disaggregated data, statisticians, researchers and individuals engaged in work with women, as well as women themselves, are being trained in gender-sensitive research, and in how to adopt and apply a gender perspective in collecting, analysing, interpreting and using all data, including census data.

In 1999 CARICOM organized a regional workshop in which 21 statisticians from several countries participated. The aim was to increase their awareness and sensitivity to, and understanding of the need for disaggregated data, and to stress the importance of collecting information about women from women, and from women and men separately, so as to make women more 'visible' in national statistics. Participants identified data needs and developed indicators for gender equality and the economy; for gender equality in education and training, health and the environment; for gender-based violence; and for assessing the role of gender in decision making and political involvement.

At the national level staff members of statistical offices in 14 countries participated in follow-up workshops to increase their sensitivity to and understanding of the importance of building a sex-disaggregated database, and were taught how to compile and analyse gender statistics. Among these national initiatives was a Working Meeting for Local Experts and Statisticians organized by the Women's Affairs Department in Trinidad and Tobago. The participants reviewed national statistics and indicators, identified and attempted to fill gender gaps in existing data collection, developed relevant country-specific, gender-sensitive indicators, and created a database disaggregated by gender.

At the micro level, women in several communities throughout the region have participated in community-based participatory research workshops organized as part of community projects. Through their participation in these workshops and subsequently through their involvement in carrying out the research in their communities many have been actively involved in collecting, analysing and interpreting research data. Moreover, by reflecting on the reality of their lives as revealed by the data, many women have become empowered and motivated to take action to improve or change their situations.

During the last decade researchers and women in the Caribbean have also been influenced by the evolving theories of gender and feminism. Feminist critiques have challenged the ability of existing theories and models to accurately reveal the various dimensions of women's reality and the role that gender plays in the construction of that reality. Feminist researchers stress the need to analyse and explore the societal structures and relationships that keep women marginalized and in positions of disadvantage. So a great deal of research now being undertaken examines the gender division of labour; the different ways in which women and men use and manage time; how they access, control and use resources; how they generate and dispose of income; what opportunities they have and what constraints they face. In the region, too, research studies have begun to focus on Caribbean men, masculinity and femininity. To date most of this type of research is being done by the Centre for Gender and Development Studies at UWI and at the University of Guyana.

In 1997 the CARICOM secretariat contracted two gender specialists to do an analysis of the census data in CARICOM countries from
a gender perspective. Using the data collected in the 1990–1 population and housing census of the Commonwealth countries, the consultants disaggregated the data by sex for demographic trends, education,
economic activity, housing and selected other themes. They computed
and compared statistics and used these as an indication of relative
advantage or disadvantage associated with either gender. They were
therefore able to identify trends within countries and make compar-
isons across countries. They also applied four gender analytical frameworks in their analysis to show their relevance and usefulness in
analysing data, and so were able in each category to identify gender gaps,
especially in relation to women's practical and strategic needs (Mondesire and Dunn 1997). This type of research activity, the first of its kind in
the region, has introduced a level of sophistication in research on
women and gender in particular, as well as in research in general.

Non-formal education and training

Non-formal education and training programmes are vehicles for
change and empowerment and for creating awareness that change is
possible. They are also tools for empowering marginalized and disadvantaged individuals and groups and for motivating them to take
action to improve and transform their situation. They are therefore
not only essential but critical to the process of empowering women
and transforming their lives. Over the last quarter century education
and training programmes have been used by government agencies and
by NGOs as a strategy for the advancement and empowerment of
Caribbean women, and large numbers of women in every country in
the region have participated in hundreds of these programmes that
were intended to raise awareness about women's issues, to integrate
women into development, to help women to acquire a wide variety of
skills, and to empower them.

Initially, in the 1970s, because reproduction was regarded as the
primary role of women, education and training programmes were

designed to prepare and equip them for carrying out this role. Formal and non-formal programmes therefore often reflected sex stereotypes and gender bias. In the 1980s, however, as the work on women developed and expanded, as changing perceptions and understanding of women's multiple roles grew, and as women's struggle for equity and equality intensified, it became clear that while all women were oppressed, exploited and discriminated against, different groups of women experienced these disadvantages in different ways. In response, the content and focus of education and training programmes changed and consistent efforts were made to design programmes to meet the needs of different groups of women. In addition to helping women to acquire skills, participation in these programmes increased women's understanding of the underlying causes of their oppression, surbordination and powerlessness; provided them with opportunities to examine and confront their position of disadvantage; and allowed them to explore strategies to gain control over their lives and to negotiate and transform their relationships with men.

Community education and training

Community-based training programmes have included those originally intended to raise consciousness about women's status and role, those intended to integrate women into development and those intended to empower women. These programmes provided opportunities for women in poor rural and urban communities to participate in a number of workshops on a wide variety of subjects and topics, and by so doing to develop self-confidence and to improve their self-esteem.

I used to be shy and afraid to speak out in a group or crowd, but since these workshops, I gained confidence and am not afraid to speak to anyone not even if the queen come.

I wasn't so sure of myself before, I was not thinking as I am thinking now. Now I see myself as more conscious, my self-esteem built up, I have more self-confidence, I want to move on.

I am somebody, I want to make him [her boyfriend] *know that I am somebody!*

In one of the workshops in a rural community, after an activity to identify skills, one woman who was a farmer exclaimed:

Today is the first day in my life that I realize that I have a skill!

As she said this she went through a total transformation, her face lit up, she smiled, she straightened her back, squared her shoulders and stood tall, and she has not looked back since. For other women participation in education and training programmes changed their approach to life and living.

Going to classes has changed my way of living into a more meaningful one.

In these programmes women acquired skills in inter-personal relations, communication, group building and teamwork. As a result many have changed their attitudes towards others, now have more respect for and appreciation of others' strengths and weaknesses, and are better able to work in groups and as part of a team to solve common problems and to achieve common goals. Through their participation in community-based education and training programmes women also developed the confidence and acquired skills that allowed them to assume leadership roles in their communities.

We women are realizing that we are just as capable as the men.

Women are showing strength and potential.

Education and training programmes intended to integrate women into development were organized within the context of community and rural development projects. In many cases the training was based on the particular practical needs of women in the communities for increased income-earning opportunities, for improved housing and sanitation, for child care and pre-school education, for improved health and nutrition, and for agricultural information and other resources. Women thus acquired skills in literacy and basic education, in problem solving, in programme planning and in evaluation.

Community-based education and training programmes based on the practical needs dictated by the situation and condition of women not only brought about change in women's lives and in the roles that they played in their communities. Another result of their participation in these programmes and their subsequent actions was that men's perceptions of and attitudes towards them also began to change.

I never thought that women could be so business-like, they are no longer the weaker sex.

Women should be treated better: they are filling a big gap in this community.

While participation in these programmes did help women to meet their practical needs, it gradually became clear that while it was necessary to focus on providing women with specific information and skills in such things as agriculture, home management, literacy, problem solving, sewing and craft, it was also important to expose them to new and different types of information and concepts in order to increase their understanding of the many complex factors that affect how they participate and benefit from national development programmes and projects. This resulted in a shift in the content, focus and process of many of these programmes: women began to reflect on, discuss and analyse topics such as the paucity of information on women's experience and reality, on women's invisibility, on their multiple roles and the changing roles of women and men, and on male–female relations. This led them to explore issues like inequality, power relations and exploitation, and to examine and analyse their own attitudes as well as men's attitudes towards these issues. As they shared their experiences and problems and described their personal struggles, and as they explored and analysed their social reality, women were better able to identify the source of women's oppression and of exploitation and discrimination against women. They also became more aware of gender inequalities within their families and communities.

Participation in these discussions and analyses became a process of learning, empowerment and change. The new awareness, knowledge and skills that women gained gave them a new vision of themselves, enabled them to articulate their needs, to express themselves with confidence, to challenge the established male order, to decrease their economic dependence on their partners and to take control of their lives.

> *I learnt that men and women are made differently and have different needs.*

> *I realize that women don't have to depend on men.*

> *I was pregnant and not working, I was dependant on my boyfriend, I had to wait on him. But since going to those workshops, I am not thinking the way I was. I see that I can move on. I have got a little job. My boyfriend is not too happy about this. He says that when I wasn't working the relationship was better.*

> *My relationship is not going anywhere, I want to end it. I don't see any future in it, I want to do something with my life.*

While the new awareness and new confidence gained through exposure to education and training gave women the courage to end exploitative relationships, it also had negative effects. For example, some men forbade their partners to participate in education programmes or to go to classes; others showed their displeasure by abusing and becoming violent to their women, by refusing to eat pre-prepared meals, and by withholding economic support.

> *On the days that I had to go to class, I would prepare supper before I left, but my husband refused to eat it if I was not there.*

> *When I got back from class, he beat me and ordered me to stop going.*

Skills training

In the Caribbean many women are accustomed to using their home-making skills in food preparation and preservation and in sewing to generate and supplement their incomes. Skills training programmes not only built on these but broadened the range of skills; they trained women in non-traditional skills and exposed them to training in small business management.

For over 40 years the Trinidad and Tobago Electricity Commission, through an organization called the Electrical Association of Women (EAW), has been training women to care for and repair electrical appliances. The Association offers regular six-week courses for women at several locations throughout the country. While the intention of the EAW was not employment but to enable women to use and care for electrical appliances bought mainly from the Commission, the Association did and still does provide women with the opportunity to acquire knowledge and skills in an area which was and is still regarded by some as male.

Concern about the high levels of unemployment among women in all countries and about their need to earn and increase their income resulted in the implementation of a large number of programmes in skills training and small business management. The realization that comparatively well-paid occupations in the technical and technological fields were mostly held by men also led to an increase in the number of programmes designed to expose women to technical and vocational education and training and to help them to acquire non-traditional skills. During the 1980s, therefore, several secondary schools and technical institutes began to open classes in construction, electricity and engine repairs to female students. National Machineries and women's NGOs also implemented a number of such training programmes and, as recently as a year ago, the Division of Gender Affairs in Trinidad and Tobago implemented a training programme in small appliance repairs and construction skills for women, especially those who were single, heads of households, and living in the poorest communities in the country.

The result is a growing number of women with skills that were once regarded as the prerogative of men, and although many still face hostility and resentment from some employers and from their colleagues and peers, the number of women now employed in male-dominated occupations is increasing.

Leadership training

Leadership training has been conducted within community-based programmes and projects as well as at national level. Within the former, women in poor rural and urban communities gained confidence and skills, and were motivated to accept leadership positions in groups and in their communities. Exposure to and participation in decision-making, planning and management processes, and opportunities to take responsibility for activities, programmes and projects, helped women to gain valuable practical experience in leadership. In evaluating one of the many community projects, however, a young woman who had participated in several community workshops, including those on leadership, remarked:

> *I had always wanted to be secretary, I know I could do it, but I never got the chance. They didn't feel I was good enough.*

This comment raises several questions about leadership training programmes, including the concept of leadership, the difference between leaders and leadership, different approaches to leadership, and how leaders are appointed or selected. It also raises the question why, in spite of so many leadership training programmes, so many women are still reluctant to accept leadership positions, and why some of those who are willing are never 'given the chance'. It also suggests that the leadership programmes have been ineffective, failing to achieve the goal of equipping and motivating women for leadership positions.

At the national level, the National Machinery and women's organizations in several countries have organized leadership training programmes for many years. Most of these programmes focus on leadership in organizations, and it is only recently that some attention has been paid to preparing women for national leadership and encouraging them to pursue and accept leadership at the highest levels of decision making.

Within the last few years Women's Leadership Institutes have been established in two countries, and so far the focus of their programmes have been on preparing women for leadership in their communities.

The Guyana Women's Leadership Institute was opened in 1998 and organizes a variety of training activities, including weekend workshops for young women, seminars on gender issues in the world of work, and training for unskilled women. A series of ten-week full-time training programmes target young as well as mature women mainly from the poor rural and hinterland communities. The programme includes modules on a wide variety of topics designed to build self-esteem, to increase the knowledge and understanding of women's issues and of gender, and to develop interpersonal, technical, communication, management and computer literacy skills. To date over three hundred women have participated in the Institute's programme.

In 2000 the Department of Gender Affairs in Trinidad and Tobago established a Women's Leadership and Enhancement Institute. The Institute aims to prepare women for personal, community, professional and national leadership. Among the activities organized by the Institute have been training programmes to build the capacity of women to take on leadership roles in their communities.

The National Organization of Women in Barbados has recently implemented a leadership training programme for its member organizations. The programme – its theme is 'Strategic Management of Women's Organizations' – is designed to equip members with skills and competencies that they need to be able to assume leadership positions and perform leadership tasks, and to improve the way in which they now manage their organizations. Within the programme women have also examined the role of women's organizations in a changing environment, and strategies for addressing women's issues and gender issues.

Training of activists

Training of activists has been an important activity in the Caribbean, and over the last decade or so such training programmes have provided opportunities for a number of women to deepen their understanding of the factors that shape their reality and that determine their experiences, to identify and highlight women's concerns and needs, and to locate and analyse their struggles for equality and equity within the geopolitical and macro-economic context. It has also provided them with new insights into the reasons for gender inequalities in their societies and increased their understanding of patriarchy. It has led individual women as well as women's organizations to question their work, to introduce new perspectives, to root their activism in feminist theory, and to see it as part of the larger struggle for women's empowerment and for the creation of more equitable and just societies.

In 1992 WAND and CAFRA jointly organized the first formal training programme for activists, the Summer Institute in Feminist Theory. Its participants were grassroots activists from across the region. Among other things they were offered modules on the global economy, feminism, sexuality, spirituality and religion. The programme, the first of its kind in the region, provided an opportunity for women working with women in communities to review and reflect on their practice, to identify and understand the links between their work and feminist theory, and to better understand the relationship between women's subordination, their unpaid and voluntary work, and the global economy.

Subsequently several activists have participated in similar training workshops and seminars. These activities usually provide participants with an historical overview of women's struggles and the women's movement internationally and in the Caribbean. In addition, in order to increase understanding of feminism and patriarchy, they expose women to feminist theory and concepts by developing and presenting them with a conceptual framework within which to position the links and relationships between these concepts, their own reality and that of other women. In this way feminist theory provides participants with a view of their own efforts as part of the larger struggle. During the training they are also introduced to new perspectives and dimensions of women's oppression and powerlessness, and they explore different approaches and strategies for advocacy work, as well as for addressing and dealing with specific issues and problems faced by Caribbean women.

Projects

Following the UN Conference on Women in 1975 and the UN Decade for Women, in the Caribbean as elsewhere a number of (mainly small) WID projects were implemented and 'women's components' were put into larger, existing projects. These projects were intended to integrate women into development and to improve the situation of women by providing them with opportunities to increase their income. While subsequent evaluation and analysis have highlighted several weaknesses and gaps, these projects did meet some of women's practical needs and significant numbers of women did benefit from participating in them.

The income-generating projects implemented in communities in several countries provided opportunities for women to use their skills to increase their earning power, and community projects with 'women's components' brought women together and enabled them to work together to solve problems, to provide services, and to improve the quality of life in their communities. Within and through the various project activities women were also able to identify their problems, concerns and needs, to explore solutions and to act to improve their situation and conditions. Traditional sewing, craft, food preparation and preservation projects mushroomed in many communities, but women also became involved in health projects, in small livestock and other agricultural projects and in integrated rural and community development projects. While several women were able to increase their earning power as a result of their participation in some of these projects, they also gained and developed skills in problem solving, in planning, in interpersonal relations and in working together. Through their participation as women they gained self-confidence, and as their self-esteem grew there was a dramatic change in how they perceived themselves.

Participating in this project has taught me a lot of things. I learnt to value me. I used to be shy and afraid to speak out, but now when I have some thing to say I say it, I am not afraid.

Before, I did not know I had skills and that all of the things I did as a housewife and farmer were skills that were important to the development of the community.

We learnt how to deal with business matters.

Because of the project we now approach our problems in a different way.

We do things in a more planned and systematic way now.

The joy of working together.

A great deal of informal communication and interrelationships at various levels, and the official contacts.

It helped women to recognize their importance and contribution to the development of their communities.

Before we women never saw ourselves as movers or as people who could get the things that they needed, done.

In some cases men resented and objected to their partners involvement in these projects, and felt threatened by the self-confidence being displayed by women, but as the projects progressed they began to realize that they, their families and the entire community were benefiting, and their views changed.

At first my husband tried to prevent me from participating in project activities, but when he saw how the family was benefiting from what I was learning, he began to help with the housework so that I could go to the meetings of the women's group.

When the project started, I was against it. I felt that it was putting the women against men, but I have come to see that what the women are doing is benefiting men in real ways.

Before I used to beat my wife but no more. If there is a problem, we now sit down and discuss it. The project is responsible for that.

By participating in the project, I was exposed to many things. I heard new ideas and began to see things differently. It made me think about how I was treating my wife and I began to change.

The women leaders in the community group are not only role models for other women but for men as well. Men see them as people with leadership skills, integrity and understanding.

Participation in many of these projects also allowed women and men in communities, in many cases for the first time, to communicate and interact with government field officers and other officials, as well as with individuals from local NGOs and from regional and international agencies.

We learnt where and how to get whatever help we need.

The project made us develop confidence in the extension worker.

We became more acquainted with resource persons, sources of assistance and procedures for dealing with them.

Within the integrated community projects women were more visible and played active roles, and in several communities it became clear that women were a powerful force for sustained community action. Moreover, as the work in many of the projects became more complex and demanding, men seemed less willing to shoulder the increasing responsibilities and several dropped out or stopped participating in project activities. In many cases, therefore, women emerged as leaders. They served as chairpersons of committees, as facilitators, and as coordinators of various project activities; they showed that they were not only concerned, but also committed to their own development and to working to develop their communities.

These projects, therefore, not only 'integrated' women into development but provided evidence that women were committed to contributing to the development of their communities in practical and concrete ways, and that the role of women in rural/community development was more substantial than was generally acknowledged. They also drew attention to the fact that while there was probably some truth in the perception of women in poor rural communities as powerless and in need of help, many of these women were capable of holding positions of power within their communities and were an important element that could determine outcomes and the success or failure of development initiatives.

Examining the process and outcomes of these community projects from a gender perspective also reveals that men seemed less willing to be involved in the development process and to contribute to it in the way women did.

Policy makers have much to learn from these projects, including the lesson that if rural and community development projects, and by extension national development initiatives, are to have the desired outcomes and impact, serious attention must be paid to the role of women in this process. This means equipping them for and empowering them to perform this role effectively.

NOTE

1 The National Machineries for the Advancement of Women have had different names over the years. In several countries the names changed as the machinery was upgraded and gained more 'status'. Among the names used were: Women's Desks, Women's Bureaux, Division of Women's Affairs, Department of Women's Affairs and Ministry of Women's Affairs. More recently, with a shift in emphasis to gender, some countries have established Bureaux, Divisons and Departments of Gender Affairs, the shift in emphasis declaring a broader brief inclusive of women's and gender issues, and addressing the concerns of men as well.

CHAPTER 6

Women, Gender, Poverty and Violence

As the twentieth century drew to a close and as many involved in working with women and on gender issues reflected on their work and looked at the challenges facing Caribbean women at the dawn of the new century, two issues emerged as being of critical importance. These are the increase in the level of poverty and its implications for women, and the simultaneous increase in domestic violence and abuse of women.

Poverty

Globalization, trade liberalization, the introduction of structural adjustment programmes, and the loss of preferential treatment for Windward Island bananas have all contributed to an increase in poverty and to a deterioration in the quality of life for a significant number of people in the region. Over the years, the banana industry has provided employment and contributed to sustainable livelihoods for large numbers of women and their families, but with its decline ...

> ... *living conditions have got worse, life is hard, it is a struggle to bring up children now.*

> *The standard of living has dropped drastically since bananas failed.*

During the last decade of the 1990s, there was a growing concern about these phenomena and about their negative impact, especially on poor people. Consequently in the late 1990s initiatives were taken to find out the extent of poverty and to develop plans and programmes to reduce and ultimately to eradicate it. Between 1996 and 2000 poverty assessments, including surveys of living conditions, were carried out in Barbados, Belize, Grenada, St Kitts–Nevis, St Lucia, St Vincent and the Grenadines, Turks and Caicos Islands, and Trinidad and Tobago.

Data from all of these assessments reveal that nearly one third of the population in several countries were poor, that poverty was more widespread among female-headed households, and that over half of all poor households were headed by women.

Table 6.1 Poverty estimates in selected countries

Country	Poor population as % of total population	Poor households as % of total no. of households	Female-headed households as % of poor households
Barbados	13.9	8.7	59
Grenada	32.1	23.8	51
St Kitts–Nevis	30.5	16.0	58
St Vincent & the Grenadines	37.5	30.6	57.9
Turks and Caicos Islands	26	26	52

Sources: Barbados, IDB (1988); other islands, KAIRI (1997, 1999, 2000).

Women and poverty

The data also show that the majority of poor women live in rural communities, have low levels of education and few marketable skills, are unemployed or underemployed, work for very low wages, and are responsible for the economic support of their families (see box, p. 119).

Poor female-headed households often consist of extended and multi-generational families that include large numbers of children, adolescents and young adults, and elderly persons, the majority of whom are unemployed and therefore dependent on the female head for all of their needs (see box, p. 120).

Profile of a poor woman

Barbara is 33 years old. She has nine children – five boys and four girls – who range in age from 18 years to six months. Three of the children have one father, four have another, and she is living with the father of the last two. He is also unemployed and when he gets a little work he will give her something, but he is violent and will beat her if she complains. She does not get anything from the fathers of the other children. The two oldest children are looking for work but so far have been unsuccessful. The oldest girl, who is 16, has just told her that she is pregnant.

Barbara did not complete primary school. She had to leave because she was pregnant. At one time she started going to sewing classes run by a community group, but the group broke up. She has been unemployed for the last year. Before that she worked at the estate factory for three years but it closed down and she has not been able to get a job since. On the odd occasion she does a little washing.

Because she has no regular income and little money she cannot afford to eat or to feed her children properly. She knows that they should eat some vegetables but they are expensive and she cannot afford them. Often her children go to school without lunch.

Neither she nor her children are in good health. She suffers from diabetes, two of the children are asthmatic and another has a growth on his neck. She and the children sometimes go to the health clinic, but she cannot afford the medicine. The doctor has told her that the child with the growth needs an operation, but she doesn't know when she will be able to pay for this.

Barbara is very unhappy and feels 'beaten down'. She feels that society does not care about her, or about whether she lives or dies.

Profile of a poor female-headed household

The household consists of nine persons, a 30-year-old woman and her five children, who range in age from 17 years to eight months, her mother, and a younger sister and brother. Although her mother lives with her, the woman is responsible for meeting all of the needs of the family, but she left school early because of pregnancy and she has no academic qualifications or marketable skills. She is unemployed most of the time. Occasionally she may get a job working on the road or she may do a little washing or ironing for someone. Her brother and sister are looking for jobs but so far have been unsuccessful. Her mother is old and not in good health but she tries to help out by selling a few sweets, biscuits, matches and cigarettes from a tray set up outside the house.

The children's father does not provide for them on a regular basis. Once in a while an aunt in England may send some money or clothes, but at other times the woman is forced to ask her sister for $5 or to 'credit' from the shop, but she does not like to buy on credit or borrow, because she can't pay back.

All of the children except the oldest and youngest are in school. The former is enrolled in a skills training programme where she is learning sewing. She is allowed to attend free because her mother cannot afford to pay the fee.

The family lives in a one-room wooden house which, although it is small and has no facilities, is better than the one in which they lived before. They have few resources and there is not enough money to provide their basic needs. Any money that is available is spent on food, but there is often not enough of that and a balanced meal is a rarity. Sometimes the children go to school without lunch. The most serious problem the family has is the inability of this single parent and head of household to find steady employment so that she can at least feed her family.

She and her family find life very hard. They 'take it how they can get it' and they make do with what they have. She is not happy or content with her life or with the conditions under which she is living but she feels that there is nothing she can do to improve or change the situation.

When women have large families children often go without adequate meals.

Interviews with women in poor households and focus group discussions with women in poor communities in several islands provided opportunities for women to describe their experience of poverty and its impact on their lives and on that of those children and families. The greatest concern of poor women is their inability to feed their children, to be able to send them to school, and to give them the things that they need.

I can't afford to feed the children properly.

Sometimes I don't eat, whatever little I get I give to the children.

I feel embarrassed when my children need something and I can't afford to buy it for them.

As a result, in an effort to see that their children are provided for, many poor women neglect themselves; their health suffers, and they are sometimes forced to engage in undesirable activities.

I don't know when last I buy a frock, I can't afford, what little money I get I have to buy food for the children.

I am not shame to say it, I does go with two, three men so as to get food for them children. It better than stealing. If I steal they will put me in gaol and then the children would starve.

Sometimes I don't have money to buy food for the children, they have to go to school without lunch.

I don't even have money to buy a box of matches to boil water to give the children a little hot water to drink.

I does worry and get headache studying about where I going to get food for them children.

Unemployment, underemployment and low wages are common among poor women. Because of low education and lack of skills they are often unable to get a job or to obtain whatever jobs might be available, and are often only equipped for low-skilled, low-paying jobs. At the same time, many women are among the working poor who, because of low wages, work at two and sometimes three jobs, but whose total income is still insufficient to meet their families' needs.

I work at a factory but the money can't meet my needs.

We need better paying jobs, especially on the industrial sites.

Finding employment is a major problem.

I work at the industrial site but the money is small so I sell cookies and so on.

Some mothers have to work at two jobs to support their families, they leave home early and return late so there is little time for family life.

I trust [take credit] from the shop and pay every week, sometimes the money is just enough to pay the shop.

I hate trusting, my heart hurts me when I have to face the shop.

We exist from week to week on small pay.

In addition, poor women in search of work are sometimes exploited by men. They are expected to give sexual favours and to put up with insults, lewd remarks and other forms of harassment.

Men who in charge of giving the work won't give work to women they can't touch up. They want to play with you first.

All stupidness have to go on, if you don't go to bed with them they don't give you no work.

In addition to unemployment, poor women also experience problems in finding and affording adequate shelter for their families.

I live in a shack, I have three small children, and I worry about the hurricane.

I need a house, there is not enough room for the children, there is not enough privacy.

Eleven of us living in this small house.

Many poor women have inherited poverty and are caught in a vicious cycle out of which they find it hard to break and from which they think it impossible to escape. They live a routine, meaningless life in a state of mental poverty characterized by powerlessness, hopelessness and frustration.

I living in poverty since I born.

Poverty is a situation where you don't have a choice.

Something missing in my life.

Poverty limit my development.

My family was always poor, from creation I come and meet them poor and they dead poor, it is the same with me and my children.

I don't see any way out of poverty, I will always be poor.

Some poor women blame the irresponsibility of men for their condition, for poor gender relations and for an unsatisfactory family life, and a growing number of poor women are victims of domestic violence and abuse from their partners.

Fathers do not do their part.

The children father don't give me any money.

I fed up with taking him to court for child support, so I decide to try and see about my children myself.

Poverty affects relationships.

My boyfriend drinks a lot and we fight often.

Men and poverty

We have seen that significant numbers of women, especially those who are single parents and heads of households, are living in poverty, and that the most severe impact of poverty is their inability to fed their children. Because the focus of attention is more often placed on the situation and needs of poor women, and because men are often seen as contributing to women's poverty, men's experience of poverty is often less examined, and its effect on them less recognized and understood. Focus group discussions with men in poor communities provided opportunities for them to share and reflect on their experience of being poor.

Like poor women, poor men also have low levels of education, lack marketable skills, and are either unemployable of unemployed. Those who are able to find employment have to settle for occasional, seasonal or part-time work, and for low wages that are insufficient to provide their basic needs and those of their families.

There are no job opportunities, you go for months without work.

I am not able to meet my commitments.

You get the money but it is so little it useless, you can't see your way.

I can't maintain the children as I should.

Being poor has severely eroded the self-esteem of many men and undermined their manhood. Unable to live up to their responsibility of providing for their families, they feel inferior and inadequate. Poverty also affects their relationships with their women and with other men.

You feel like a dog when you poor, especially if you have to wait for people to give you something. You can't feel like a man.

It brings conflict in the home and breakdown in families.

When I have nothing to give, I can't go by the woman and sleep.

I have to hide to buy a drink or buy it and take it home because I can't afford to buy for the fellas.

Several men also said that being poor left them feeling frustrated and angry and often led them to indulge in drugs or to become violent.

I get angry and frustrated 'cos times so hard.

When a man don't have work and no money he could rob or kill.

You have to do things you don't want to do, like drugs and crime.

Research has clearly shown that poverty affects men and women differently, that they react to and deal with it differently. While women's main concern is their inability to feed their children, men's is their inability to provide for their families and to meet their commitments. Poor men said that being poor eroded their manhood and their status as 'real men', and had a negative effect on their relationships with other men. However, while poor women admitted that poverty sometimes had a negative affect on their relationships with men, it did not affect their relationships with other women in the same way. Men and women also reacted to and coped with poverty in different ways, including involvement in illegal activities: prostitution for women and drugs and violent crimes for men.

In addition, poor women and men employ a number of strategies that help them to cope and that ensure their survival. They do a number of odd jobs to help themselves; they use their few resources wisely; and they often depend on relatives and neighbours for clothes and other things. While some are forced to resort to begging, many are also willing to share and to help and support each other.

Initiatives and interventions to tackle poverty

Poverty reduction is a priority of most governments in the region, and several have implemented alleviation and reduction programmes. In Trinidad and Tobago the Small Business Development Company is government's vehicle for stimulating micro and small economic enterprises. Ninety per cent of the participants in the scheme have been women and 80 per cent of those who participate in its Community Venture Programme are women (National Country Report 2000). In

Grenada, Dominica, and St Vincent strategies for poverty alleviation and reduction include rural enterprise projects, the Basic Needs Trust Fund and human resource development programmes in which there is supposed to be a focus on poor women and on female-headed households. In all countries NGOs and women's groups have also implemented programmes and projects designed to improve living conditions in rural communities, and within these activities there is usually a focus on women. However, research needs to be done to assess the differential impact of these initiatives on poor men and poor women.

While these initiatives are steps in the right direction, in many cases planners and field officers in the government departments that are responsible for the poverty alleviation and reduction programmes are not gender sensitive, have not developed skills in gender analysis and gender planning, and have little expertise or experience in using participatory approaches and methodologies. Many of these programmes and projects have not been informed by accurate and specific data about poor women and poor men in the rural communities in which they are to be implemented. Consequently, poverty reduction programmes and projects are being developed and implemented without an understanding of the realities of poor women and men, or of the effect that gender relations can have on their participation and on the benefits that they might derive from these initiatives.

Violence against women

In all Caribbean countries there is a growing concern about the increase in violence of all types and particularly about the apparent increase in the incidence of violence against women, as well as about the increasing brutality of this violence. However, society's attitude to this phenomenon is still somewhat indifferent and many individuals are still of the view that it is a private, family affair. Because of this, bystanders may look on as a man beats a woman in the street; a bruised and battered women is treated with indifference when she makes a complaint to the police ; and few of the male relatives who rape young girls are ever brought to justice.

In the Caribbean there is also still a great deal of ambivalence about sexual harassment and there are those, mainly men but some women too, who say that 'touching and fondling are signs of affection and are part of Caribbean culture'. However significant numbers of women have experienced sexual harassment in the workplace, on the streets and in other public places. As a result, in recent years sexual harassment, abuse of women and domestic violence have been included in training sessions and workshops, and there have been several marches and demonstrations against offences of this kind.

While the growing concern and agitation about violence against women has led governments in the region to take some action to address the issue, many women and women's organizations across the region are still of the view that neither governments nor the population at large is giving abuse and violence against women the serious attention that it deserves. In Barbados, for example, while there is currently some discussion on the introduction of a Bill on Sexual Harassment, women and women's organizations feel that progress on this matter is too slow. At a recent march and rally organized by the National Organization of Women (NOW), several women and a few men, concerned about the urgent need for this legislation, bore placards calling for sexual harassment laws to be introduced immediately. At the end of the rally, at which the deputy prime minister was present, the president of NOW presented a list of issues about which women were concerned and for which they were requesting immediate action by the government.

Because of the persistence of traditional beliefs about women's role and place in society and about male–female relationships, and because of the response of duty officers, many women who experience violence and abuse are reluctant to make reports to the police, and because data in police records are not disaggregated by sex, it is difficult to obtain accurate statistics on gender-based violence. There is therefore little 'hard data' on the incidence of abuse and violence against women in the region. In an attempt to fill this gap, in recent years a number of research studies on this issue have been carried out in several countries. These studies provide information about the various types of violence which women experience, about the victims' experiences, and about responses by the police and other judicial agencies, and by women's organizations.

Research on violence

Between 1986 and 1989 research conducted by the Women's Affairs Department in St Vincent and the Grenadines revealed that 75 per cent of the perpetrators of violence against women were males in common law relationships, 15 per cent were husbands and 10 per cent other male relatives. It also showed that the majority of victims were single, unemployed women between the ages of 13 and 34 (St Vincent and the Grenadines 1995).

In Barbados between 1987 and 1989 the Bureau of Women's Affairs commissioned a study on the incidence of domestic violence (Jordan 1999). The results of this study were used to introduce legislative reform. In St Vincent and the Grenadines between 1989 and 1991 the National Machinery undertook a similar study to determine the status of domestic violence (St Vincent and the Grenadines 1995).

In 1988 Women Against Violence in Belize conducted a study on the nature of violence against women. The study collected data on the cases reported to the police and to medical departments, and on the number of cases processed in the criminal courts. In 1993 records on domestic violence cases showed that between May and November, 103 cases had reached the courts (Report on the Status of Women 1994). A 1991 study in Dominica stated that only 13.9 per cent of women who said that they had experienced domestic violence reported it to the police. In Guyana this figure was 5.9 per cent.

Reasons given for this low level of reporting include women's belief that they had caused or been responsible for the violence, and that they therefore deserved it; their belief that that is men's way of showing who is in charge; their fear of repercussions; and their economic dependence. In addition, many female victims of violence feel that even if they report it to the police nothing will be done. This is borne out in the Guyana study, where in only 10.6 per cent of reported cases of domestic violence was the offender charged. Further, in one third of the reported cases, the offender was warned and in 25 per cent no action was taken against the offender (Clarke 1998).

A study in Barbados (Ellis 1998) found that the staff of the Probation Department comes into contact with a significant number of young girls who have been abused and who are living in environ- ments that put them at risk. Yet when these girls 'run away' from home they are charged with 'wandering' or with 'being a girl under the age of 16 found in circumstances calculated to cause or encourage seduction and prostitution'. The staff expressed concerned about the number of these young girls who appear before the courts for leaving home.

A situational analysis of gender-based violence in St Lucia (Francis 1999) revealed that 398 females and 89 males contacted the Crisis Centre in 1993, and that by 1996 the numbers had increased to 460 females and 99 males. It also showed that the most commonly reported type of domestic violence was spousal abuse, and that between 1993 and 1996 there was an increase of 33.9 per cent in the number of these cases reported. In terms of rape and indecent assault, 153 cases were reported in 1997, an increase of 34 over the number reported two years earlier. The study also indicated that most of those contacting the Centre were between 20 and 39 years of age (*ibid.*).

CAFRA is currently conducting research on the incidence of domestic violence in the region, the first stage of which is a pilot study with 200 women in Trinidad.

Reports of violence and abuse against women

It is generally recognized that the number of cases of violence that women report are only a fraction of those that take place, and that those reported are not representative of their number or severity. A look at statistics on domestic violence and at police and other reports of violence against women shows that women are victims of a wide variety of violent crimes and especially of domestic violence, including verbal, emotional, physical and sexual abuse, incest and rape. In Trinidad and Tobago between 1996 and 1998, for example, figures on murders resulting from domestic violence show that 73 per cent of the 51 victims were women; and of the 64 women murdered by men in Jamaica in 1993, over half were between 13 and 30 years. In St Vincent and the Grenadines between 1989 and 1992 there were several gruesome murders of females.

Police reports of rape show that in Barbados over the period 1985–9 there were 229 reports of rape; over the same period 412 cases were reported in Guyana and 909 in Trinidad and Tobago. In Jamaica during the five-year period 1988–92 a total of 5,253 rapes were reported to the police and there were 328 calls and visits from rape victims to the Crisis Centre. Other calls to the Centre included 134 for incest and 692 for domestic violence (Report on the Status of Women 1994). In Anguilla between 1990 and 1993 there were 317 reports of domestic violence, 436 in the Bahamas and 4,673 in Trinidad. Police records in Trinidad and Tobago for 1991 show that a woman was raped every 1.75 days. In Jamaica in 1993 there were 1,297 cases of rape and carnal abuse; 38 per cent of the victims were between the ages of 18 and 25 years and 44 per cent of the cases were in relation to carnal abuse against girls under 16 years of age. The 1993 statistics also show that 52 boys appeared before the court charged with rape and other sexual offences (Clarke 1998).

There is a concern, however, that even when violence against women is reported, only a small number of the cases reach the courts; even more rarely are charges laid or convictions secured. The St Vincent research referred to earlier found that of the 702 reported cases of domestic violence only 15 per cent of the offenders were actually convicted, and of the 2,522 reports of rape made in Barbados, Guyana, and Trinidad and Tobago between 1985 and 1989, only 809 charges were laid and 115 convictions handed down. Of 323 cases of sexual abuse before the court in Jamaica, 115 resulted in conviction, 112 were not prosecuted and 96 of the offenders were acquitted.

Women's experiences

The stories of women who are victims of abuse and violence tell of the range of brutal acts, describe the cycle of violence, and etch in the trauma and devastating effects on their lives. The following snapshots have been created from and contain the words of some female victims of abuse and form 'true stories' told by the victims, social workers and counsellors to researchers. They give an idea of the scope and seriousness of violence and abuse against women and an appreciation of the experience from the victims' point of view.

Snapshots of abuse and violence against women

Intimidation, threats, ridicule

When she wants sanitary napkins she has to ask her husband.
You want more of those again? Where are the ones I bought you last time?

He insults and ridicules her in public with comments like:
You so stupid, you don't know anything, why you don't shut your mouth when big people talking?
You are no better than a whore.
If you tell anybody I'll kill you.

Some male police officers, bailiffs and magistrates insult and ridicule victims with comments such as:
Why you don't stop nagging the man? You get what you deserve.
You get the man in trouble, you satisfied now?

Economic abuse

She has not been allowed to touch or spend money for years, she recently tried to commit suicide.

Her salary goes straight into a joint account but she can't withdraw any of it, her husband spends it as he sees fit.

She depends on him for financial support, but if she doesn't have sex with him he won't give her money.

He refuses to support the children so she goes from man to man hoping to get a few cents to buy food for them. In the process she becomes pregnant, and the cycle continues.

➤

Physical abuse

Her mother beat her regularly as a child and now her partner does the same.

Her man chopped her with a cutlass because he said she had another man.

Her partner beats, slaps and kicks her regularly and tells her that she deserves it because she is no good.

He beat her so bad that she is now disfigured.

She was six months pregnant but he kicked her in her belly and she lost the baby.

He burnt her on her face and put her hands in the fire because the food was not ready.

He held her by her hair and threw her across the room, then threw a chair at her while her two-year-old son watched and cowered in fear.

When he come home drunk he does beat me real bad.

They were married for 27 years and during that time he has broken practically every bone in her body, yet she is afraid to leave him, because he has told her if she tries to leave he will kill her.

Sexual abuse

She was sexually abused by her uncle when she was ten, at 16 she was raped by her mother's boyfriend.

Sexually abused as a child, raped at 20 and again at 32, she is still receiving counselling.

At age 40 she was raped at knifepoint in her own bed by an intruder while her children slept in the next room.

> *My stepfather interfering with me since I small but my mother won't believe me; I can't stand it no more.*
>
> She is 12 years old and has run away from home four times to get away from beatings from her mother and sexual abuse by her mother's boyfriends.
>
> She has six children from three different men. She was beaten regularly by all of the men.
>
> She was the victim of incest from age 12, she was raped on the streets, contracted AIDS and died before she was 25.

Response to violence against women

While there is now a greater willingness to report crimes of violence against women, the majority of victims are still ashamed and afraid to admit to being a victim or to make reports to the police. Women's reluctance to contact the police or to report acts of violence and abuse against them is often an indication of their acceptance of violence as part of their life and of their lack of trust and faith in the police and the judicial system. The response of the police to domestic violence was originally, and is still to some extent characterized by an attitude based on the belief that it is a family affair and that they should only intervene if it becomes too serious. Generally they do not take husband and wife disputes seriously and they do not encourage wives (women) to take their husbands (men) to court.

The long and humiliating interrogation, the slow and long court process, and the small number of offenders convicted all deter victims from taking legal action and together perpetuate and reinforce women's reluctance to access the judicial system. Society's reaction and response to domestic violence and women's dependence on men for financial and emotional support ensure that many victims remain in bondage.

This situation has led to women and women's groups to agitate for changes in the law and in the judicial system, in the court processes, and in the attitude of police, lawyers, magistrates and judges. As a result there is a growing recognition of the need for greater advocacy against violence towards women and a need to provide a wide range of support services for the victims. Consequently, since 1985 governments and NGOs have undertaken a number of initiatives at national and regional level to address and deal with the problem. Among these have been new legislation and legal reform; mechanisms to support female victims of violence and abuse; meetings, rallies and demonstrations; conferences and seminars; education, training programmes and documentation.

Government initiatives

Legislation and legal reform

In the late 1990s the CARICOM Women's Desk developed model legislation with respect to domestic violence. Using this, several countries have undertaken law reform and introduced new legislation to deal with domestic violence.

In 1985 the Magistrate's Court (Domestic Proceedings) Ordinance was passed in Turks and Caicos Islands. In Trinidad and Tobago the Sexual Offences Act was passed in 1986 and the Domestic Violence Act in 1991. In 1999 both of these acts were amended: the Sexual Offences Amendment Act provides a new definition of rape and says that a husband could be charged with the rape of his wife. In the Domestic Violence Act No. 27 of 1999, among other reforms, the definition of domestic violence was extended to include psychological and financial abuse. In Barbados, the Sexual Offences Act and the Domestic Violence (Protection Orders) Act were passed in 1992, and made provision for the police to intervene once they suspect that an individual is being physically abused. In 1995–6, 142 requests for protection were made and granted. In Belize the Family Court was established in 1989 and a Domestic Violence Act was proclaimed in 1993. In St Lucia, while there is no legislation dealing specifically with sexual harassment, the Domestic Violence Summary Proceedings Act 1994 deals with cases of domestic violence and the Criminal Code through the Sexual Offences Act deals with rape, indecent assault, battery, prostitution and sexual offences. A Family Court was established in 1997 and during the period June–December in that year 106 cases of domestic violence were lodged, and 199 cases in January–September the following year. Family courts also exist in Belize, Grenada, Jamaica, and St Vincent and the Grenadines: while these deal mainly with family matters like child maintenance, they have begun to handle domestic violence cases.

While there have been some significant attempts to introduce new legislation and amend existing laws to deal with violence and abuse towards women, reform has not always been easy or without its detractors. In Trinidad and Tobago, for instance, the first draft of the Sexual Offences Bill had made rape within marriage a criminal offence; in spite of wide support from women and women's organizations, however, by the time the Bill was passed, marital rape was criminalized only in cases where the parties had been separated for at least two years or where there were court proceedings to effect a separation. The withdrawal of the wider clause on marital rape was the result of united opposition from male members of parliament and male lawyers and clergymen, and of the exclusion of the public from parliamentary debate on the Bill.

Other government initiatives

In recognition of the need to provide support services for victims of domestic violence, Special Units have been created within the police services in Barbados, Jamaica, St Kitts–Nevis, and Trinidad and Tobago. In Barbados a Victim Support Unit was established in 1995. Staffed by volunteers, it provides counselling services to victims of rape and child abuse, and prepares them for their appearance in court. In Jamaica Sexual Offences Investigation Units are located in every parish where, in addition to recording statements and keeping records for court matters, they provide a range of services to victims and organize public education programmes on domestic violence. In 1989 in St Kitts–Nevis a Delinquency Unit was formed and part of its mandate was to deal with reported cases of domestic violence and to provide counselling to victims. In Trinidad and Tobago there is a Juvenile Bureau and Counselling Unit that handles rape, abuse and incest; within the police service, Community Policing Units have been established to deal with social issues, especially domestic violence, and legal aid is now available to victims of domestic violence. In Trinidad and Tobago, too, a central registry has been created to collect data on domestic violence. In 1995 the Family Services Section in the Welfare Department, Barbados, organized a training seminar on domestic violence for its officers.

In Belize, Barbados, Guyana, and St Vincent and the Grenadines the National Machineries have organized seminars to increase public awareness of the incidence of violence against women and have organized training programmes for social workers, police and other law officers to increase their sensitivity and understanding of the cycle of violence and to develop their skills in how to deal with and treat female victims of domestic violence. In St Lucia and Barbados they have also published and distributed posters, pamphlets and booklets on domestic violence, rape and incest, and have presented pro-grammes on radio and television. In Dominica, and St Vincent and the Grenadines the Machineries and Social Welfare Departments also offer counselling and advice to female victims and, occasionally in severe cases, have even given them financial support.

NGO response and initiatives

To a large extent it has been through the work of NGOs that the issue of violence and abuse of women has been receiving more attention and that actions are being taken to address it. Women's organizations have implemented and sustained a number of programmes to raise public awareness and to work towards the elimination of domestic violence. In addition, in the last two decades, new organizations with a special focus on eliminating gender-based violence have emerged in several countries. Among these are the Committee for the Eradication of Violence in St Kitts, Women Against Violence in Belize (1985), the Group of Concerned Women in Grenada, Help and Shelter, a counselling centre run by CAFRA in Guyana, the National Committee Against Violence in St Vincent and the Grenadines, and a National Coalition on Domestic Violence in Trinidad and Tobago. A new phenomenon, too, is the emergence of men's groups which, like Men Against Violence Against Women (MAVAW) in Trinidad and Tobago, are focusing on the elimination of gender-based and domestic violence.

Women's organizations throughout the region continue to lobby for legislative reform to address domestic violence. They have implemented public education and awareness campaigns, candlelight vigils, marches and rallies, training activities, including sessions in schools, special projects and special events on the International Day Against Violence Against Women in November

Advocacy

Women's organizations throughout the region have been very vocal about the high incidence of abuse and violence against women, and have been unrelenting in their demands to their governments, the police and the judicial services to take decisive action to address the issue and to deal with the perpetrators. They continue to lobby for legislative reform and new laws to protect women from abusive partners and to increase sentences against convicted offenders. Organizers and participants alike have made speeches and used poetry, music and drama to draw the attention of policy makers and the public to the plight of victims and their need for support services, as well as to the cost of domestic violence to the country. These activities have increased awareness of the incidence of violence and have highlighted the increasing brutality of these crimes.

While this has often been a difficult and onerous task, and while the response to their demands has not always been what was expected, their persistence has had some positive results: in several countries, as we have seen, new and amended laws have been passed and protection orders institutionalized.

Campaigns

Between November 1997 and December 1998, UNIFEM's Latin and Caribbean Office organized a Campaign on Violence Against Women to raise public awareness, to disseminate information about the high incidence of violence against girls and women in the region, and to sensitize and motivate governments to develop and/or change policies, legislation and practices to prevent violence against women. The campaign was organized within the context of the United Nations Inter-Agency Campaign on Women's Human Rights. The first activity in the Caribbean – billed as 'A Life Free of Violence: It's Our Right' – was a meeting of women's NGO crisis centres in which 22 women representing crisis centres in 11 countries participated. They planned and designed the campaign and appointed CAFRA to coordinate and supervise it. Other activities included radio and television programmes, a telethon, rallies, marches and vigils, seminars and workshops, newsletters and posters.

The final event in the campaign was a Regional Tribunal on Violence Against Women, held in Barbados on 20 November 1998. The Tribunal focused on domestic and sexual violence against women and girls, child abuse, sexual harassment and abuse of women's reproductive rights. During the day 14 women from several Caribbean countries shared their experiences of being victims of domestic violence and abuse with a large audience. A Tribunal comprised of a panel of lawyers and judges from different countries heard their stories and passed judgements, while members of the audience were given opportunities to respond to the testimonies and to discuss the issues. In order to support the victims and to enable them to tell their stories, they were counselled prior to the event and arrangements were made to have a 'comfort room' with a team of counsellors and psychologists available to the women during the meeting and afterwards.

The women's stories were compelling and moving. The audience were brought to a new realization of the degree of brutality displayed by the perpetrators; the cool response of the police; the ineffectiveness of the judicial system in convicting offenders and imposing lenient sentences on those who were convicted; the feelings of guilt, agony and despair felt by the victims; and the obvious physical and emotional scars which the experience had left on them.

Supportive mechanisms

Women's organizations have also created a number of mechanisms to provide support for female victims of violence and abuse. Among these are hotlines, crisis centres, shelters and drop-in centres that offer information, advice and counselling (see Figure 6.1, p. 140).

Projects

NGOs have also used projects as a strategy to address the issue of violence against women, to demystify the law, and to inform and educate women about ways to deal with abuse and violence.

In 1990 the Caribbean Women Trade Unionists' Membership Education Project was implemented. Within this project, a regional women's writing team, comprised of women from different trade unions across the region, developed and wrote several handbooks. Among them was one entitled *Caribbean Working Women Against Sexual Harassment: a Handbook for Trade Unionists*. The handbook, piloted and discussed in study circle sessions, was published in 1996 by the Commonwealth Trade Union Council. Topics covered in the handbook include: 'What is Sexual Harassment?', 'Dealing with Sexual Harassment', 'Is Sexual Harassment a Trade Union Issue?', 'Sexual Harassment and the Law' and 'Finding Solutions to Sexual Harassment'.

In 1999 the Ministry of Women's Affairs in St Lucia, with financial assistance from the Canadian International Development Agency (CIDA), implemented a project on 'Combating Gender Based Violence'. The project was intended, among other things, to increase public awareness, to sensitize the judiciary, police, media and other key groups in the society, and to train some individuals in intervention methods and techniques, and in counselling skills.

Among the activities undertaken were a situation analysis of

Figure 6.1 Support mechanisms for victims of domestic violence and abuse in selected countries

Country	Hotlines	Crisis centres	Shelters for abused and battered women	Drop-in centres offering information, advice and counselling
Bahamas		Women's Crisis Centre		
Barbados	BPWC Hotline	BPWC Crisis Centre	Shelter for Battered Women (BPWC & Government)	PAREDOS Churches WAND
Dominica	DNCW Crisis Hotline	Crisis Relief Centre		Dominica National Council of Women
Grenada	Group of Concerned Women, Rape Crisis Hotline			Legal Aid and Counselling Clinic
Guyana			Help and Shelter Ltd	CAFRA Counselling Centre
Jamaica		Women's Crisis Centre	Women Inc. (established 1989)	Women's Crisis Centre
St Lucia		Women's Crisis Centre (established 1988)		
St Vincent			Halfway House	Marion House
Trinidad and Tobago	National Domestic Violence Hotline, 24 hrs, 7 days a week, for victims and perpetrators	Rape Crisis Society	Five shelters for battered women	Available in 22 communities

gender-based violence, a public education and information dissemination programme, community consultations and meetings, sessions in schools, training of police and community groups, sessions with media workers, the establishment of community response teams, discussions with the Ministry of Legal Affairs and the development of a proposal for the establishment of gender violence units within the police services. The implementation of these activities provided opportunities for agencies and social institutions involved in dealing with gender-based violence to share experiences and to explore ways in which they could collaborate to continue these activities and to sustain the momentum beyond the project period.

Over the last decade or so, CAFRA has implemented a number of regional projects that focused on and addressed issues related to violence against women. Activities in these projects included research, training and documentation (see Figure 6.2 on p. 142).

Education and training

Training in domestic violence has been undertaken at the regional and national level with women, men, law enforcement officers and social workers. Public education and awareness-building programmes have been organized in several countries to raise awareness and increase understanding of and sensitivity to the existence and incidence of domestic violence, to draw attention to the strategies being used to address the problem, to identify and discuss the social and economic costs to individuals and society, to identify the gaps in services and to examine possible solutions. The National Machinery, women's organizations, and regional and international agencies have organized conferences, seminars and training workshops in several countries on abuse and domestic violence against women.

In 1988 Women Against Violence in Belize organized a national conference on family violence ('Violence Behind Closed Doors') and in the same year the Caribbean Human Rights Network, in collaboration with several NGOs and the police force, organized a seminar on domestic violence in Barbados. Among the 50-odd participants were

Figure 6.2 CAFRA'S projects on abuse and violence against women

Year	Projects/activities
1987-98	Regional research project on Women's Rights and the Law in collaboration with the Inter-American Legal Services Association.
1989-93	Women and the Law Project, implemented in eight countries.
1991	Regional meeting on Women, Violence and the Law, in collaboration with the United Nations Economic Commission for Latin America and the Caribbean (ECLAC) and the Rape Crisis Centre, Trinidad.
1992	Paralegal training for 85 women activists.
	Published *Domestic Violence and the Law*, an educational booklet on the Trinidad and Tobago Domestic Violence Act (1991).
1993	Legal education workshops and public forum on Violence Against Women in four countries.
1995	Published booklet on *Child Support, a Need, a Must: Getting Child Maintenance in the Magistrates' Courts*.
1997–8	Implemented UN Inter-Agency Campaign on Women's Human Rights (A Life Free of Violence: It's Our Right) in collaboration with UNIFEM.
1999–2001	Regional training programme on domestic violence for police officers and social workers.

the director of the Bureau of Women's Affairs, psychologists, counsellors, police officers, teachers, students, welfare officers, media workers, the ombudsman, a magistrate, and members of women's groups and organizations.

Popular theatre methods – drama, song, poetry and dance – are also used in training workshops and seminars as a strategy to discuss and examine abuse against women and domestic violence, and to highlight the police response to these and to the victims. In the Barbados seminar, a skit by popular theatre animators highlighted the cycle of domestic violence from verbal to physical abuse, and pointed out the reason why victims remain; it also suggested ways in which the victim could leave the situation and turn her life around. In Jamaica, Sistren Theatre Collective conducts popular theatre workshops on violence against women on a regular basis, and in Trinidad popular theatre presentations on family and domestic violence have been conducted in secondary schools. A full-length drama (*Shades of I She*) that examines domestic violence through drama, music, poetry and dance has also been presented in several countries and attended by large audiences.

Audio-visual materials, including posters, leaflets, booklets and videos, are also used in education and training programmes. Among these are videos on abuse, harassment and domestic violence, including *The Alarm Rings Softly*, produced in Trinidad and Tobago for the Fourth World Conference on Women, and *Smart Young Man*, one of four vignettes on a video produced by the Ministry of Culture and Gender Affairs in Trinidad. The latter is used as a discussion starter in sessions with various groups. Leaflets and booklets include *Stop Rape*, *Myths about Battered Women* and *Say No To Sexual Violence*.

Training the police

During two general assemblies (1998 and 1990) of the Association of Caribbean Commissioners of Police, presentations were made on 'Violence Against Women and the Role of Police'. The presentations drew attention to the negative reaction and attitudes displayed by some police officers to complaints of domestic violence, to their reluctance to intervene, and to the undesirable ways in which they responded to and dealt with female victims of abuse and domestic violence. As a result, the commissioners agreed to implement and support training programmes for police officers.

Consequently, over the last five years or so, there has been a marked increase in the number of regional and national-level programmes intended to sensitize police about issues related to domestic violence and abuse against women, to expose them to tecniques and methods for intervening in situations of domestic violence, and to equip them with skills in investigating violence and abuse against women and in dealing with victims of domestic violence.

The Regional Police Training Centre in Barbados trains recruits and senior police officers from countries in the region, and in 1999 it conducted a two-week domestic violence training course out of which was developed a *Manual on Management of Domestic Violence and Counselling*. The manual has been piloted and revised and will be used by the Centre in its training of police officers in the various countries. Training of police officers and members of the protective services and of the judiciary has taken place in several countries, and the Ministry of Culture and Gender Affairs in Trinidad and Tobago has organized workshops for police officers and for new recruits in the coast guard, including the first battalion of female recruits. One of the topics discussed was 'Managing Gender Conflicts'. The National Coalition Against Domestic Violence, at the request of the police commissioner, also conducted training workshops for four hundred police officers, and a gender consultant conducted a session on domestic violence for superintendents and other senior officers in the force. Similar training for police personnel is now being undertaken in Antigua, Barbados, Belize, Dominica and Guyana.

With financial support from the international and regional funding agencies, and in collaboration with the Association of Caribbean Commissioners of Police, in 2000 CAFRA implemented a regional project entitled 'Domestic Violence Intervention for Police and Social Workers'. The project aimed to train 26,000 officers and a number of social workers to increase their understanding of the cycle of abuse and of the factors that contribute to and perpetuate abuse and domestic violence, and to enable and better equip them to be able to intervene in domestic violence situations.

Activities undertaken with the project included the production of a domestic violence training manual, a regional 'training of trainers' programme, and national training of police officers and social workers by the trained trainers. The manual was pilot tested during the training of trainers programme, in which eight senior police officers and four social workers from eight countries participated. In the second phase of the project these 12 trainers trained two hundred officers and social workers in how to use the manual and prepared them to train others on returning to their own countries.

CHAPTER 7

Men's Issues
and the Issue of Men

While the emergence of a focus on men's issues is seen by some as a male backlash and as the negative reaction of Caribbean men to the advances made by women over the last three decades, it is now being recognized that in order to transform gender relations and to achieve a more equitable, just and humane society it is important to acknowledge that men also have issues and to pay some attention to them.

Feminist activists and gender and development specialists have come to realize the importance of paying attention to men's issues.

Like Caribbean women, Caribbean men are not a homogeneous group but are divided by race, social class, status and education level. However, at all levels of Caribbean society men appear to be having difficulty in accepting the gains made by Caribbean women in the last 25 years and in adjusting to changing gender roles and relations.

Male marginalization and discrimination against men

The idea that Caribbean men are marginalized emerged out of research on *The Marginalization of the Black Male* (Miller 1991) and the author's definition of marginalization as being constantly on the periphery of power, wealth and status, and being unable to make decisions that are beneficial to you.

Marginalization of Caribbean men is seen to be the result of several interrelated and complex factors, including the conflict and competition between men and women for power, changing societal norms and values, the construction of masculinity and femininity, gender segregation, and the erosion of the traditional role of the male as breadwinner, provider and protector. While some men have acknowledged that the absence of adult males as role models in the home and school, the two most important institutions of socialization, has contributed to deviant behaviour and lack of responsibility among men, many blame women for these phenomena.

A lot of deviant behaviour by young boys and girls is a result of women's behaviour towards their children's fathers.

Among the explanations given for the marginalization of men are the women's movement, the increase of opportunities and benefits for women, the growth of feminism, and the quest for gender equity and equality. Many men are therefore of the opinion that as women have progressed men have become alienated; they feel powerlessness and experience despair and hopelessness. Consequently, men as well as women throughout the region have participated in many public and private debates and discussions that attempted to find out and explain if and why Caribbean men are at risk or in crisis. Emerging from these activities have been ideas and statements suggesting that, while men still believe they have the right to exert power and control over women, they have been adversely affected by the loss of power, authority, control and respect, have become alienated, and feel confused and frustrated. Unable to deal with feelings of inadequacy, or to cope with changes in gender roles and relations, or to redefine their roles, especially in relationship to the 'new' Caribbean woman, several have attempted to regain power by turning to domestic violence.

Men have also begun to speak out about oppression and discrimination. For example, in Trinidad and Tobago in 1998 there were 418 reports of domestic violence against men. At a men's forum convened by the Child Care Board in Barbados in 2000, over three hundred men shared their experiences of being abused by women and of being refused access to see and interact with their children.

In Trinidad and Tobago, in order to address the issue of domestic violence, the Department of Gender Affairs established a male support committee. Initially the committee dealt with matters related to domestic violence, but its work has expanded to deal with other issues affecting men and their relationships with women. Its activities include the provision of support to vulnerable men, and working with men's groups to resocialize boys and men.

Many men are also of the view that the legal system favours women and discriminates against men, especially in the areas of child maintenance and the custody of children, the terms of visiting rights and the framing of protection orders. They feel that the courts are ruling in favour of women, that women are using the courts to exploit and take revenge on men, and that women who sexually abused young boys are seldom brought to court or prosecuted. Moreover they blame this state of affairs on the increase in the numbers of female lawyers and magistrates.

The woman tells me that she will get a house out of me through the court.

Women who sexually abuse boys and engage in sexual activity with under-aged boys are not brought to justice.

A large number of men and some women still believe that the women's movement is anti-male and actively seeks to marginalize men. In response to this, in addition to men's groups, some women's groups and other NGOs have since the late 1980s organized activities to sensitize men about women's position, condition and concerns, and to focus equal attention on men's role in society and on their relations with women.

Gender identity, masculinity and femininity

Societal expectations and socialization play a major role in shaping people's perceptions of manhood and womanhood. As a result men and women usually perform the roles and display the attitudes and behaviours that their society expects of them. Research conducted in Barbados and St Vincent revealed that several people were of the view that masculine and feminine identities are decreed by God, and that gender differences are biologically determined. Several are also still convinced that men and women possess different and distinct qualities that are natural to their sex and that enable them to perform the specific gender roles for which they are intended and which society expects of them. As the following comments show, women as well as men, and young as well as older people hold these views.

Men and women are built differently. (Male, 46–55 years)

Women are soft and more understanding, they are also more emotional, they are made that way; but men need to be strong to carry out their responsibilities. (Male, 20–30 years)

Strong aggressive women are tomboys. (Female, under 20)

There is a growing understanding, however, that while gender is about masculinity and femininity, it is much more than that. Gender is about recognizing the importance of human relationships; it is about examining how history has shaped and defined both women and men; and about how men as well as women have assisted in defining male and female behaviour. Moreover, gender relations are not limited to relationships between men and women, but include relationships between men and men and between women and women as they relate to and interact with each other.

Caribbean men, masculinity and manhood

In the last few years, as more programmes focused on gender roles and relations, there was a feeling that in too many cases men were being blamed for all of women's problems. They were being excluded, and their problems were being neither recognized nor heeded. Many men therefore feel threatened by the advances made by women; others are confused, angry and defensive; and some are venting these emotions by displaying undesirable behaviours. This male backlash has had several significant outcomes, some positive, and some negative.

On one hand there has been an intensification of public debates and discussions as well as seminars on topics such as 'Are Caribbean Men in Crisis?' or 'Irresponsible Caribbean Men: Fact or Fiction?' In 1996 the Centre for Gender and Development Studies at UWI organized a three-day symposium on the topic 'Caribbean Masculinities'. On the other, several research studies are now being undertaken to generate new knowledge and insights into masculinity and to get men's views about what it means to be a 'Caribbean man'. Among the research topics are 'Marginality and the Caribbean Male', 'Masculinity, Ethnicity and Identity' and 'Men and Domestic Violence'.

A significant amount of work is also being done on the role of men in the family as spouses and fathers, and on socialization practices and patterns. In 1993 the UWI Child Development Centre in Jamaica carried out a study to find out how males and females in the Caribbean are socialized into specific gender roles, and how this determines the type and quality of male/female relationships (Browne and Chevanes 1998). This participatory research project, implemented in 1993, was carried out over a period of two years in six communities: one in Dominica, two in Guyana and three in Jamaica. Central to the research process data collection were the discussions in which groups of men and women in each of the communities shared their experiences and gave their opinions on a number of pertinent topics. Several major themes emerged form these discussions. One of these was the regional version of manhood.

The concept of Caribbean manhood

Community members were clear about what constituted manhood and identified as important elements sexuality, sexual identity and fertility, and man's ability to provide for the family. They subscribed to the belief that man is supposed to be head of the family and to have authority over women and children. Moreover, many saw such authority as natural and part of God's plan. It is instructive that these traditional beliefs still exist and are perpetuated even by women who have been single parents and heads of households for many years.

Research data revealed that man/woman relationships are characterized by distrust and disillusionment, infidelity, power and authority of the male, domestic violence, sharing of housework, and the belief that the man is the financial provider.

A man who cannot provide for his family is not a man.

The data also show that relationships between men and women are affected by economic factors, and by the high level of unemployment and underemployment among men and women in poor communities; and that different and contradictory messages about sexuality and sexual identity are given to boys and girls. Socialization and traditional child-rearing practices also reinforce gender distinctions by disciplining boys differently from girls, and by emphasizing that leisure activities are more acceptable in boys and that social skills and values are more desirable and acceptable in girls.

The role of men in the family has long been a matter of concern for many Caribbean women and the popular stereotype of the 'irresponsible Caribbean man' has been believed for a long time because of the large number of absentee and visiting fathers. However, data from this project revealed that men were more involved in family life and contributing more to family life than popular stereotypes suggested; that there is a small but growing number of single-parent households headed by males; and that an increasing number of younger men appear to be taking their parental responsibilities seriously, becoming actively involved in child care and child rearing.

The findings of this research project were shared through symposia in each of the three participating countries, and in 1996 a radio drama series, entitled *How Men Really Feel* and based on the research findings, was aired on radio stations throughout the region. This project is an important initial step in generating information about and insights into the experience and feelings of men, of the constraints and challenges that they face as they attempt to 'be a man' and to perform their roles in a constantly changing environment. It has also increased understanding of how gender socialization has and can contribute to gender role conflicts and unharmonious male–female relationships.

New men's groups

In response to the women's movement a men's movement seems to be evolving in the Caribbean. Feeling threatened by women's progress, afraid of 'women taking over', and recognizing that one way to address men's issues is through organized groups that can lobby for change, men are getting together in groups and creating spaces and opportunities for men to express their emotions, views and opinions. These new groups can be identified along a continuum that reflects different phases and stages in the development of the movement. At one end are those groups whose focus is still on blaming women and on trying to turn back the clock, and on the other are those that are more concerned with understanding the factors that are responsible for and that perpetuate gender inequalities and discrimination.

Within this context a great deal of emphasis is being placed on men's needs and on issues that are of concern to them. Issues of male domination and their apparent loss of power, of women's progress, of gender inequalities, of male marginalization, of manhood and fatherhood, of male responsibility in the family, community and society, of male–female relations and of domestic violence, and of male performance in the education system – these are the topics that have focused the attention of men's groups.

Fathers' groups

The common practice of casual sex, multiple partnerships and absentee fathers are three factors that contribute to the large number of female-headed households – and to the belief that Caribbean men are irresponsible.

Fathers Incorporated

The group originally called 'Fathers Only' was founded in 1990 by seventeen young men, ages 25-35, who participated in a 'men only' workshop during a conference on parenting organized by the Caribbean Child Development Centre at the Mona Campus of UWI.

Through its work it drew attention to the important role that men have to play in the family and as fathers, and within two years of its creation its membership grew to over one hundred, and it changed its name to Fathers Incorporated.

Concerned about the negative image, attitudes and behaviours of Jamaican men, and about the prevailing stereotype of the absentee and irresponsible father, the group's aim is to help men to become better fathers. It mobilizes and trains men to act as peer counsellors, and it uses drama-in-education to elicit men's views about fatherhood and to inform and sensitize them about their role in the family and as fathers.

In addition to workshops on fatherhood, the group has also organized workshops on male—female relations and on sexuality. In these fora, male-only participants discuss, among other things, condom use and traditional attitudes towards sex.

Members of the group have also appeared on radio programmes and have 'played fathers' to children in various institutions.

While fathers as well as mothers' groups have existed in St Lucia for several years, within the last few years in several other countries, for example in St Kitts and Jamaica, a number of new male groups have emerged and are focusing on the role of men as fathers. Workshops are also being held to provide opportunities for men to discuss parenting and their roles as fathers, and to examine their relationships with their children and with their children's mothers.

In 1990 a group of young fathers in Jamaica, concerned about the attitude and behaviour of men in the family and in the wider society, formed a group with the aim of projecting a more positive image of fatherhood, improving men's self-image, and changing the attitudes of Jamaican men (see box on p. 153).

Activist groups

Within the region there are a few activist groups whose activities and programmes focus on addressing men's issues and on topics such as marginalization and discrimination against men and gender-based violence, and whose activities include sensitizing and providing support for men and agitating for change in laws and societal structures. Two of the most vibrant and active activist organizations are the Men's Education and Support Association (MESA) in Barbados (see box on p. 155) and MAVAW in Trinidad and Tobago (see box on p. 156). While MESA's agenda is broad-based and seeks to address several issues that are of concern to men, MAVAW has a more specific focus and is concerned with gender relations and with the elimination of gender-based violence.

During the last half of the last decade of the last century the Caribbean has witnessed the beginning of what some refer to as a men's movement. There is a general belief among Caribbean women that this phenomenon has been influenced by, and is a reaction and a response by Caribbean men to the activities of Caribbean women and women's organizations, and to the dramatic progress made by the former in all areas of life and work.

As Caribbean men and men's groups struggle to understand, to come to terms with, and to accept changing gender roles and relations and the redistribution of power among men and women, they would be well advised to reflect on Caribbean women's experiences and struggle over the years; to examine their strategies and to learn from their successes and failures. In doing so they need to view strong, progressive and competent women not as a threat but as an asset, and to commit themselves to working hand in hand with them for a more equitable and just society.

Men's Education and Support Association (MESA)

The Men's Educational Support Association was founded in Barbados in 2000, and is open to all men 18 years and over. Its motto is 'Stronger Men, Stronger Families, a Stronger Society'.

Its objectives are to provide a forum for males to share experiences and ideas, to serve as a support group for men, to educate males about their roles and responsibilities as spouses, fathers and citizens, and to empower them so that they are better able to share leadership roles in the family and the society.

To date MESA has held several meetings and discussions in different locations throughout the country and contributes a weekly column to one of the daily newspapers dealing with issues of concern to men.

Its programme is implemented through a number of sub-committees and at present the legal sub-committee is investigating the law as it relates to the relationship between parents, especially fathers, and their children. It has initiated a great deal of discussion on the proposed changes in the family law and has questioned whether these changes will benefit women by discriminating against men. The health sub-committee plans seminars, panel discussions and lectures on prostate cancer, stress management, substance abuse, mental health, and AIDS awareness and prevention. The counselling sub-committee provides advice and referrals.

MESA is extremely active. Its strategy of mobilizing men takes it into communities all over the country and it has been able to motivate large numbers of men to participate in its various activities and discussions. Its activities are highlighted in the media and it has approached government for a subvention to enable it to continue and expand its work with and for men.

Men Against Violence Against Women (MAVAW)

Men Against Violence Against Women is a group of male activists in Trinidad and Tobago. The idea for the group emerged in a forum on the rise in crime hosted by the National Women's Caucus, and its creation was based on a decision to have a crime committee comprised of concerned men. This committee, with an initial focus on the violent behaviour of males and on developing strategies to reduce and eliminate crime, eventually developed into MAVAW.

The organization's goal is to reduce and eventually eradicate violence against women and it aims to promote male responsibility in achieving this objective. It has developed a code called The Promise of Responsible Orderlies in which men make promises to God, the nation, the family and themselves: members of the organization see it as a mechanism that provides a proactive way for men to take responsibility for violence and to work towards the creation of a non-violent society.

MAVAW's strategies include sensitizing men about their responsibility and reaching and providing support for men who are in violent relationships, who are in denial, who are in distress, and who are trying to change their violent behaviour.

During the first five years of its existence, MAVAW implemented a large number of programmes including several seminars, workshops and panel discussions, a male awareness week, and a weekly one-hour, call-in radio programme entitled 'Talking Gender'.

Topics covered in the latter included 'The Growth of Feminism and the Perceived Male Backlash', 'Coping with Family Conflicts', 'Gender Equity', 'Gender Socialization' and 'Gender and Religion'. The programmes were intended to raise men's consciousness and awareness about gender issues, especially about domestic violence; and to create, train and equip committed and professional men to provide counselling and support to men and women involved in violent relationships.

CHAPTER 8

Gender and Development

The Women and Development approach introduced in the 1970s produced strategies intended to integrate women into development. However, in the mid-1980s, analysis of the existing development models, influenced by DAWN and employing a feminist perspective, led to the realization that the current paradigm of development and many of the development models being used were dominated by male opinion and by masculine patterns of behaviour. This led many women's organizations to search for and experiment with alternative models and approaches that would empower women rather than integrating them into existing patriarchal models.

The examination and analysis of two decades of work based on the concept of Women in Development highlighted the fact that women's reality is to a large extent determined and influenced by their relationships with men – their fathers, brothers and other male relatives, their spouses and male co-workers. Moreover, the realization that men and women participate in the development process and benefit from development initiatives in different ways from men also drew attention to the fact that the social relations of gender in the family, community and workplace were important factors that determined outcomes.

Over the last decade or so – as people tried to understand the factors that shape masculine and feminine identities, that determine gender roles, and that influence how men and women relate to each other – there was a shift in focus from *women*, and the issue of *gender* assumed a great deal of importance. The growth of the women's movement and concern about women's condition and position of disadvantage *vis-à-vis* that of men in their societies led to the recognition that these phenomena are the result of a fundamentally unequal distribution of power among men and women, and of existing societal structures, arrangements and procedures that reinforce and perpetuate gender inequality. It was also realized and affirmed that gender discrimination and oppression is counterproductive: the achievement of gender equity and equality is not only desirable, but is also critical to the achievement of development goals.

Race, class and gender often define the pattern of working relations. The introduction of the concept of gender and its use as an analytical tool, like race and class, has therefore helped to increase and to deepen understanding of the difference between sex and gender and of the social relations of gender. It has also helped policy makers and programme planners to see the importance of understanding social reality from the perspectives of women as well as of men. In addition, when gender is used as a tool to examine, analyse and interpret social reality, the experience of women as well as of men is validated. An understanding of gender is also essential to an understanding of the factors that contribute, reinforce and perpetuate women's subordination and oppression.

Consequently, a great deal of the work that is now being done on gender in the region is focusing on the identification and examination of the many ways in which men and women interact and relate to each other, and on analyzing how gender relations determine and influence personal, community, organizational and national development. In addition, gender analysis is helping to increase understanding of how, why and in what ways the development initiatives affect, benefit and impact on men and women.

Over the last decade, there have been several debates and discussions on gender and development and on changing gender roles and relations, and to some extent these have helped to increase understanding of the importance of and the need to focus on gender issues. However, many men and women are still confused by the debates and discussions, and are unclear about the meaning of gender, about gender roles and relations, and about what are gender issues.

We have covered a little ground but people still don't understand it [gender].

What is it all about? People still believe in the Bible and that man is the head of the household.

Up to now people have not grasped the concept of gender.

It's how gender was introduced.

Yet the debates and discussions on gender have touched the lives of men and women at all levels of Caribbean society and have resulted in an increase in understanding of what gender is, of how it is linked to individual, community and national development, and in a more rational approach to the discussion of women's and gender issues.

Gender is about masculinity and femininity, but it is much more than that, it is about recognizing the importance of human relationships.

Gender is not just about how men and women define themselves in society but it is also about relations between men and women, and between women and women.

Women cannot continue to lag behind men, men haven't got all the answers, there are two sexes and we must work hand in hand.

If we want to change society, we need fresh blood and a mixing of the genders.

On the other hand, because in the region the word gender, like the word feminist, has negative connotations for many people, the debates and discussions on gender and gender issues have also generated several negative emotional responses, including resentment, anger and hostility – mainly from men, but also from some women. Many people are still confused about the relationship between women's issues and gender, and in the minds of many, gender and gender issues are still interpreted as women's issues.

This gender thing is just another way for women to get what they want, to disrespect and rule men.

Gender inequality is a dominant aspect of reality that contributes negatively to Caribbean development. Discussion of the concepts of gender equality and gender equity have identified the need for alternative development models and approaches, and for a new paradigm of development that is based on a code of justice for all, a gender-sensitive approach to development planning, and the development and implementation of policies and programmes that respond to the needs of women as well as of men.

Women and men participating in various fora and activities in the region have pointed out that the present paradigm of development is dominated by the views and opinions of men, and that it therefore cannot guarantee gender equality. In 1990 a study on 'The Place and Role of Women in Organizations in St Vincent and the Grenadines' pointed out that issues relating to gender equality are important to organizations that are trying to adopt alternative approaches to development (Committee for the Development of Women 1990). At a regional workshop on women and development in 1990, participants from 15 development agencies agreed that if development programmes were to address and facilitate the development of Caribbean people, it was essential to focus on gender issues as well as on women's issues, needs and concerns. At a regional economic conference held in Trinidad in 1991, representatives of NGOs pointed out to government officials that the current dominant economic development model that emphasizes economic growth was exploitative and dehumanizing to the majority of the region's people and especially its women.

In 1995 the CARICOM secretariat developed a Draft Policy on Gender Equality and Social Justice that identified several principles essential to the process of transforming gender relations and to achieving gender equality and social equity. Among these are the recognition and acceptance that women must be able to take their place alongside men and to participate in all societal processes including political decision making and policy formulation at the highest level.

Strategies to increase gender sensitivity

The shift in focus from Women in Development to Gender and Development has led to a number of initiatives, programmes and actions that highlight the importance of understanding the formation of gender identity, changing gender roles and relations, and the link between these and the achievement of national development goals. As a result, in all Caribbean countries steps have been taken to develop and implement gender-sensitive policies, strategies and programmes.

Gender-sensitive policies and programmes

Governments as well as NGOs have formulated policies and are implementing programmes and projects to increase sensitivity to gender issues, to deepen understanding of the factors that contribute to gender inequality and discrimination, and to incorporate a gender perspective into their work. In some countries former Departments of Women's Affairs have been renamed Departments of Gender Affairs and a few are staffed by men as well as by women. In St Kitts–Nevis a National Gender and Development Plan (1996–2000) is an integral part of the country's macro-economic strategy. It identifies strategic goals and specific action priorities, describes the role and function of the gender management system, of an inter-ministerial committee, of 'gender focal points' and of the National Advisory Committee on Gender Equality and Equity. The Plan was informed by a number of activities including an Equality Forum on International Women's Day in 1999, in which 98 persons including representatives from 43 organizations participated.

Among the key strategies adopted and being used to increase gender sensitivity and to promote gender equity and equality are gender training, gender planning and gender mainstreaming.

Gender training

Because a large number of men and some women are still of the view that the women's movement is anti-male and that it actively seeks to marginalize men, some women's groups and other NGOs have, since the late 1980s, organized training activities to sensitize men about women's position, condition and concerns, to increase men's awareness of their role in society, and to provide an opportunity for them to examine their relationships with women.

In 1983, the women of Rose Hall, a small community in St Vincent, expressed concern about the low participation of men in activities implemented as part of the pilot for the Integrated Rural Development Project. In response, a three-day workshop on 'The Role of Men in the Development of the Community' was organized. Among other things, the men who participated in the workshop examined their relationships with women, the Women in Development activities that were taking place in the community, and the effects of these on them, on their families and on the community as a whole.

In 1991 women in Dominica who participated in a Women's Encounter and in a workshop on women in health expressed concern about the difficulty of communicating women's concerns and gender issues to male spouses and friends. As a result the Small Projects Assistance Team (SPAT), a local development group, organized a Men's Encounter. The aim was to sensitize men working in SPAT, and in projects supported by it, to women and gender issues, and to provide them with an opportunity to share their thoughts and views about the women's movement. Among the topics discussed were men in the home, women's issues and gender issues, images of men and family planning.

Unlike some of the earlier consciousness-raising programmes that sought to increase awareness about women's role and contribution to their societies, and training programmes in which women began to examine male–female relationships, gender training focuses attention on the factors that contribute to the inequalities that exist between women and men in society and that determine and influence gender relations, on gender oppression and discrimination. It identifies and examines the societal structures, arrangements and processes that reinforce these, and that perpetuate unequal power relations and gender inequalities; it also helps policy and decision makers and programme planners to view reality through a gender lens, and to acquire and develop skills in gender analysis and gender planning. It is able to do this because it increases and deepens understanding of the difference between gender and sex, of the social relations between men and women, and of social reality in the experience and perspectives of women as well as of men.

In the last decade of the last century there was a dramatic increase in the number of training programmes, courses, workshops and sessions that had gender as their main focus, and during this period gender training became a part of the landscape in practically every country in the region; courses were also on offer at the regional level. In 1992 CIDA funded a research study on gender training in the region. Carried out in ten countries, the study reviewed and assessed the amount, type and quality of the training being conducted and the material being used; it also identified the individuals, organizations and institutions that were offering and providing the training.

Those who participated in the study saw gender training as a strategy and as a vehicle for increasing gender sensitivity, for providing information on gender issues, and for the acquisition of skills in gender analysis and gender planning. They also said that participation in gender training activities helped to clarify gender concepts and definitions, challenged societal values, norms and belief systems, and helped to translate the academic discourses on gender into practical strategies for enhancing gender relations (Pat Ellis Associates 1993).

Whereas Women in Development (WID) training was implemented largely at the community level and engaged women's and community groups and practitioners in the field, a significant amount of gender training activities have been organized for individuals at middle and senior positions in the public and private sectors. However, by participation in gender training programmes women and men at all levels of Caribbean society have obtained concrete information about the different realities of men and women, have examined child-rearing practices, gender socialization, gender stereotyping, gender roles and relationships, and the gender division of labour. At gender training workshops and sessions the analysis of power relations, power sharing and the unequal distribution and allocation of resources between men and women have helped participants to understand how gender inequality can jeopardize the process of personal, community and national development. As a result participants realize the need for strategies and actions to achieve gender equity and equality.

Gender training has taken place at all levels in Caribbean society, in communities, in organizations, in government departments, in the universities, at national and at regional levels. At the macro level, training for policy makers and planners in the public sector has been carried out in several countries so as to increase their understanding of the relationship between gender and the process and outcomes of national development, and to expose them to strategies, methods and techniques for incorporating gender into development policies, plans and programmes. Gender training has also been carried out in public and private sector organizations and in NGOs in the voluntary sector. For example, in 1995–6 the Department of Gender Affairs in Trinidad and Tobago implemented a one-year programme on 'Training and Sensitization in Gender and Development'. Programme activities included a number of training sessions and workshops for members of the cabinet, and for key individuals in various government ministries, in the judicial services, in the private sector and in NGOs. Outputs of the project included a 'training of trainers' process, the production of a gender training manual and a video that examines how gender behaviours are shaped. Gender training workshops have also been conducted with organizations and workers at all levels in the agricultural sector. Among these was a workshop for agricultural extension officers on how to build gender-sensitive activities into extension programmes. In St Lucia between 1993 and 1995 the staff of the Women's Affairs Department, members of the inter-ministerial committee, police recruits and development workers all participated in a series of gender training workshops. This training was intended to help participants create and maintain gender-sensitive environments in their organizations. Gender training workshops have also been conducted at the micro level in several communities throughout the region.

Initially, because of the perception that gender training was just another aspect of the 'women's thing', the majority of participants were women and usually organizations would send junior members of staff to such events. Within the last few years, however, more men and more women in middle and senior management positions have began to participate in these activities Because of the amount of gender training that has taken place individuals and organizations have become more informed about and more aware of the importance of gender, and of the need to address issues, to change attitudes and to transform gender relations in creating gender-sensitive environments.

Gender analysis and gender planning

Like ethnicity and class, gender can be used as an analytical tool to increase understanding of and to gain deeper insights into social reality. More specifically, it is being used to identify factors that influence the social relations between men and women, to examine critically the different experiences and perspectives of men and of women, and to recognize the ways in which these determine their participation in societal processes and the benefits they derive from national development initiatives.

Gender analysis is part of the search for new ways to achieve gender balance, gender equity and gender equality in development programmes and projects, within organizations and in society at large. Using gender as a tool of analysis increases understanding of the complexities and difference in the lives of men and women. It identifies and examines the causes of the inequalities between men and women and provides policy makers, planners and programme implementers with an opportunity to identify and examine the root causes of social problems, providing them with an alternative way of looking at social phenomena and of identifying and examining factors that shape these phenomena from a female as well as from a male perspective. It is a tool that can also be used to identify the structural causes of disadvantage and powerlessness that women experience.

Equipped with new information and deeper insights acquired from gender analysis, policy makers, planners and programme implementers are better able to appreciate the different roles played by men and by women at the micro, household and community levels, and to understand the link between these, the outcomes of national development initiatives, and the effect that macro-economic policies have on women and men in households and communities. They are then in a better position to formulate policies, to develop plans and to design programmes that are gender sensitive. Incorporating gender sensitivity in development planning, especially in the public sector, nevertheless remains a challenge to policy makers and planners.

In 1990 the CARICOM secretariat organized a regional workshop in gender analysis. The participants, who were representatives from planning departments and National Machineries in 11 countries, were exposed to a number of skills and learnt how to use a matrix to incorporate gender into national policy and national development plans. Since then, workshops to teach policy makers and planners methods and techniques, and to equip them with skills in gender analysis, have been conducted in several countries among government officials, managers in the private sector and in NGOs. It is not only important, however, to see gender analysis as a strategy for providing deeper insights into social relations and as a tool to be used in development planning in order to realize equity and equality; it is equally important to institutionalize it in the processes of all societal institutions and organizations.

Gender planning is an approach to development planning that recognizes the inequalities between men and women and attempts to identify and address the different needs of men and women. The information obtained from gender analysis is the basis for gender planning and allows planners to link the experiences and needs of men and women at the micro, household and community level to macro-level national policies and plans.

Gender mainstreaming

Gender mainstreaming is a process that attempts to address gender inequalities by transforming existing development plans and processes so that gender equality is achieved and that women are empowered and equipped to participate actively alongside men in all societal processes, including at the highest levels of policy and decision making. As elsewhere, in the Caribbean the concept of gender mainstreaming was introduced in the late 1990s and triggered discussions and debates about its meaning and relevance to Caribbean societies. Questions were and are still being asked about its purpose, about how to do it, and about whether mainstreaming gender into existing models of development can really lead to gender equality and equity. While the debates are going on some countries have undertaken activities intended to mainstream gender.

In Trinidad and Tobago some initiatives have been taken to incorporate a gender perspective into national policies, plans and programmes: among these is the presence of representatives from the Department of Gender Affairs on national committees and the revitalization of the inter-ministerial committee in 1998. In St Lucia a National Advisory Committee on Gender and Development was also established in 1998 to advise the Minister of Women's Affairs on all issues relating to women, gender and development.

In 1996 St Kitts–Nevis was selected to be part of a Commonwealth project in gender mainstreaming. Within this pilot project several activities were conducted. Among these was a survey in which 350 persons were asked their views about the work of the Ministry of Women's Affairs and to identify areas of concern; the development of a gender management system; and the establishment of a National Advisory Council on Gender Equality and Equity. The gender management system is intended to create a network of structures, mechanisms and procedures within the existing framework and to guide, plan, monitor and evaluate the process of mainstreaming gender into all government policies, plans and programmes in order to achieve gender equality and equity

An extensive process of consultation allowed representatives of various government departments and NGOs, including women's groups, youth groups, community groups, senior citizens and persons with disabilities, to identify and discuss issues of concern and to make recommendations and suggestions that would inform the creation of the gender management system and the National Gender and Development Plan.

While it is now more widely recognized that gender is a key issue that must be taken into consideration when formulating development policies and plans and programmes, it has been more difficult to translate the rhetoric about the importance of gender into policies that improve Caribbean women's condition and their position of disadvantage *vis-à-vis* that of Caribbean men, and into programmes that meet the specific needs of men and women in Caribbean society.

While there have been some attempts to integrate gender into policies and programmes of some government departments, of NGOs, and to a lesser extent within private sector agencies, there have been no attempts to assess the impact of these on men and women, or to evaluate the extent to which they have contributed to greater gender equality and equity. Probably because there is not yet a critical mass of individuals within government departments who have acquired the skills and have the commitment, gender planning is not yet widespread and far-reaching enough to really make a difference in how policies are formulated and plans and programmes are developed, designed and implemented. The region still awaits its era of structural change and transformation of administrative systems or management processes to create gender-sensitive environments and to encourage and support gender equality and gender equity.

Bibliography

ACCA (1988) *Business Education Survey in Selected CARICOM Countries.* Association of Canadian Community Colleges and the Caribbean Association of Technical and Vocational Education and Training.

Antrobus, Peggy (1989) 'Gender Implications of the Development Crisis', in Norman Girvan and George Beckford (eds), *Development in Suspense. Selected Papers and Proceedings of the First Conference on Caribbean Economists.*

—— (1990) 'Structural Adjustment: Cause or Curse? Implications for Caribbean Development', in *Bulletin of Eastern Caribbean Affairs*, Vol. 16, No. 1, Institute of Social and Economic Research, University of the West Indies.

—— (1992) *Gender Issues in Agriculture and Rural Development: A Critique of IFAD Projects in the Caribbean Region*, Women and Development Unit, University of the West Indies.

—— (2000) 'The Rise and Fall of Feminist Politics in the Caribbean Women's Movement 1975–1995', unpublished paper.

—— and Andaiye (1991) 'Towards a Vision for the Future: Gender Issues in Regional Development', paper commissioned by the West Indian Commission.

Babb, Cecilia (1998) 'Situational Analysis of Gender, Women and Poverty in the Windward Islands', unpublished draft, United Nations Development Fund fo Women, United Nations Development Programme.

Bailey, Barbara (1999) *'Issues of Gender and Education in Jamaica: What About the Boys?'* Education for All in the Caribbean Assessment 2000, Monograph Series No. 15, UNESCO.

Barbados, Government of (1990) *Population and Housing Census 1990.*

—— (1995) *Report to the United Nations Fourth World Conference on Women*, Government of Barbados, Beijing, China.

—— (1995) *White Paper on Education Reform. Preparing for the Twenty first Century. Each One Matters: Quality Education For All.* Ministry of Education, Youth and Culture, Bridgetown.

Barrow, Christine (1998) 'Barbados', in Sylvia Chant and Cathy McIlwaine (eds), *Three Generations, Two Genders, One World: Men and Women in a Changing*

Century, Zed Books, London.

Barrow, Lorna (1996) 'Women, The Invisible Minority: An Evaluation of the Present Status of Women in the BWU and Recommendations for Change', unpublished Research Paper, Centre for Gender and Development Studies, University of the West Indies, Cave Hill Barbados.

Belize, Government of (1995) *Report for the Fourth World Conference on Women, (Bejing 1995)* Government of Belize.

Belize Organization for Women and Development (BOWAND) (1994) *Women in the Garment Industry in Belize*, Belize Organisation for Women and Development.

BIDC (2000) *Review of Employment Trends in Selected Sub-Sectors. December 1999*, Barbados Investment and Development Corporation, Bridgetown.

Blackman, John (2000) article, *Sunday Sun*, 9 April.

Brown, Janet and Chevannes, Barry(1998) *Why Man Stay So? An Examination of Gender Socialisation in the Caribbean*, University of the West Indies, Mona, Jamaica.

Caribbean Association of Feminist Research and Action (CAFRA) (1988) *Women in Caribbean Agriculture: Research /Action Project: Overall, Project and Summary of Main Findings*, Caribbean Association of Feminist Research and Action.

—— (1998) *Research on the Impact of New Trade agreements on Rural Women: Preliminary Findings of a Sample of 200 Households in Dominica, Grenada, St. Lucia and St. Vincent and the Grenadines*, Caribbean Association of Feminist Research and Action.

—— (2000) 'The Absence of Rage', in *CAFRA News* Vol. 14, No. 2, Special Issue on Violence Against Women (October).

Cargill Technical Services Ltd. (1998) *Socio-Economic Impact of Banana Restructuring in St Lucia Vol. 1 Final Report*, London.

Caribbean Community (CARICOM) (1988) *Survey of Technical and Vocational Education and Training*. CARICOM Secretariat, Georgetown, Guyana.

—— (1990) *Report on the Regional Workshop/Seminar on Gender Planning and the Formulation of National Plans of Actions*, CARICOM Secretariat and the Commonwealth Secretariat.

—— (1991) *1990–1991 Population and Housing Census of the Commonwealth Caribbean*, CARICOM Secretariat, Georgetown, Guyana.

Central Bank of Barbados (2001) *Annual Reports 1999–2001*.

Clarke, Roberta (1998) *Violence against Women in the Caribbean: State and Non-State Responses*, United Nations Development Fund for Women and Inter-American Commission for Women.

Committee For the Development of Women (1990) *Unmasking The Barriers: A Survey on the Place and Role of Women in Organisations in St. Vincent and The Grenadines*, Committee for the Development of Women, The National council of Women, The National Youth Council, and Projects Promotion. Kingstown, St Vincent.

Commonwealth Secretariat (1997) *Fifth Meeting of Commonwealth Ministers*

Responsible for Women's Affairs 1996, Trinidad and Tobago.

Commonwealth Trade Union Council (1996) *Caribbean Working Women Against Sexual Harassment: A handbook for Trade Unionists*, Commonwealth Trade Union Council in the Caribbean.

Coppin Addington (1996) 'An Analysis of Earnings in Barbados by Age and Sex', *Central Bank Review*, Vol. XX111, No. 3 (December).

Cuales, Sonia (undated) 'Caribbean Young Women and Perceptions for the Future', , unpublished paper.

Drayton, Kathleen (1995) *Gender Issues in Education: A Review of the Major Gender Issues in Education and of Relevant Caribbean Studies*, Organization of Eastern Caribbean States (OECS), Castries, St. Lucia.

ECLAC (1996) *Poverty Eradication and Female-Headed Households (FHH) in the Caribbean*, Economic Commission for Latin America and the Caribbean/ Caribbean Development and Cooperation Committee.

Ellis, Patricia (1987) *A Case Study on Women in Agriculture and Rural Development in Antigua*, Women and Development Unit (WAND).

—— (1993) 'Agricultural Policies and Projects: The Need For a Gender Perspective', unpublished paper.

—— (1990) *Measures Increasing the Participation of Girls and Women in Technical and Vocational Education and Training: a Caribbean Study*, Commonwealth Secretariat, London.

—— (1998) 'St Vincent and The Grenadines', in Sylvia Chant and Cathy McIlwaine (eds), *3 Generations, 2 Genders, 1 World: Men and Women in a Changing Century*, Zed Books, London.

—— (1998) *Feasibility Study of a Shelter for Abused Females*, Soroptomists International of Jamestown, Barbados.

—— (2000) *Assessing Pockets of Poverty in the OECS/Windward Islands*, United Nations Development Programme.

Evans, Hyacinth (1999) 'Gender Differences in Education in Jamaica', in *EFA Caribbean: Assessment 2000*, Monograph Series No. 12, UNESCO.

Food and Agriculture Organization (FAO) (1991) *Women in Agriculture: The Impact of Technology on the Productive Activities on Women in Latin America and the Caribbean*, Food and Agriculture Organisation.

Francis, Aurelia Jacintha (1999) *A situational Analysis of Gender-Based Violence in St Lucia*, Gender Affairs Department, St Lucia.

Gittens, Eugene and Manigo, Sabrian (1986) *Attitudes Towards Non Traditional Work Among Grenadian Women*, Women's Affairs Department, Ministry of Health, Grenada.

Goddard, Gillian (1995). 'Inclusion and exclusion in Caribbean Feminist Organisations', in *CAFRA News*, Vol. 9, No. 2 (July–December).

Greene Cecilia (1990) *The world Market Economy: A Study of Enclave Industries in the Eastern Caribbean and Its Impact on Women Workers*, Caribbean Peoples Development Agency (CARIPEDA).

Guyana, Government of (1995) *State Paper on Education Policy*, Ministry of Education, Georgetown, Guyana.

Harvey, Ena (1993) *Report on a Workshop on Gender Analysis. First Consultation of the Caribbean Sub-Region Technical Cooperation Network of Institutions and Agencies in Support of Rural Women*, FAO.

International Labour Organization (ILO) (2000) *Small Enterprise development in the Caribbean*. ILO Studies and Working Papers No 3. ILO, Port-of –Spain, Trinidad 2000.

—— and CARICOM (1995) *Women, Labour and the Law: A Caribbean Perspective*.

Inter American Bank. (1998) *Poverty and Income Distribution in Barbados 1996– 1997. Economic and Sector Study Series*. Inter-American Development Bank.

Jamaica National Preparatory Commission (1994) *National Report on the Status of Women in Jamaica*, prepared for the Fourth World Conference on Women. Beijing, China, September 1995.

KAIRI Consultants Ltd (1997) *Poverty Assessment and Training, Final Report: Belize, St Lucia, and St Vincent and the Grenadines*.

—— (1999) *Poverty Assessment Report: Grenada*.

—— (2000) *Poverty Assessment Report: Turks and Caicos Islands*.

—— (2000) *Poverty Assessment Report: St Kitts and Nevis*.

Kelly, Deidre (1986) 'St Lucia's Female Electronic Factory Workers: Key Components in an Export-Oriented Industrialization Strategy', in *World Development*, Vol. 14, No. 7.

Knudson, Barbara and Yeates, Barbara (1981) *The Economic Role of Women in Small-Scale Farming in the Eastern Caribbean*, Women and Development Unit, St Lucia.

Leo-Rhyne, Elsie, Bailey, Barbara and Barrow, Christine (eds) (1997) *Gender: A Caribbean Multi-Disciplinary Perspective*, Ian Randle Publishers, Kingston, Jamaica.

Miller, Errol (1980) *Marginalization of the Black Male: Insights from the Development of the Teaching Profession*, Institute of Social and Economic Research, University of the West Indies, Mona.

—— (1991) *Men at Risk*, Jamaica Publishing House, Kingston, Jamaica.

Massiah, Joycelyn (1998) *On the Brink of the New Millenuum: Are Caribbean Women Prepared?*, the 1998 Inaugural Lucille Muir Lecture.

Mondesire, Alicia and Dunn, Leith (1995) *Towards Equality in Development: A Report on the Status of Women in Sixteen Caribbean Countries*, CARICOM Secretariat, Guyana.

—— (1997) *An analysis of Census Data in CARICOM Countries from a Gender Perspective*, CARICOM Secretariat, Georgetown.

Moore, Winston and Whitehall, Peter (2000) 'Financing Small and Micro-Businesses in Barbados', in *Central Bank of Barbados Economic Review*, Vol. XXV11, No. 3 (December).

Organization of Eastern Caribbean States (OECS) (1991) *Foundation for the Future: OECS Education Reform Strategy*, Organization of Eastern Caribbean States Secretariat, Castries, St Lucia.

Parris, Rennie (2000) 'A Study of Some Factors that Help or Hinder the

Participation of Women in the Construction Sector in Antigua and Barbuda', un published research paper, University of the West Indies.

Pat Ellis Associates Inc. (1993) *An Assessment of Gender Training in the Caribbean*, Canadian International Development Agency (CIDA).

Planning Institute of Jamaica (1997) *The Labour Market Newsletter*, No. 24, Kingston, Jamaica.

Reddock, Rhoda (1990) 'The Caribbean Feminist Tradition', in *Woman Speak*, Nos 26 and 27, Women and Development Unit (WAND).

'Report of a Seminar on Domestic Violence', Barbados 1998 (unpublished).

Republic of Trinidad and Tobago (1997) *Statistics and Indicators of the Status of Women, 1990–1995: Bulletin No. 1, Women's Economic Activity, Labour Force and Income*, Central Statistical Office, Port-of-Spain.

Republic of Trinidad and Tobago (2000) *National Country Report on the Status of Women*, Government of Trinidad and Tobago, Port-of-Spain.

Ross-Franklin, Joan (1990) *Facing the Issues as we Enter the 90s: Report of the CARIPEDA Workshop on Women in Development*, Caribbean People's Development Agency (CARIPEDA).

St Bernard, Godfrey (1995) 'Household and Family Structure in Contemporary Trinidad and Tobago: Implications of Research Findings', unpublished paper.

St Kitts-Nevis, Government of (1996) *National Development Plan: Gender and Development, 1996–2000*, Ministry of Women's Affairs, Basseterre.

—— (1998) *Learning and Growing: The Long Term Education Plan, 1998– 2001*, Ministry of Education, Basseterre.

Stuart, Evelyn, 'The Jamaica Women's Political Caucus 1992–1998', unpublished paper.

St Vincent and The Grenadines, Government of (1995) *Report on the Status of Women in St Vincent and the Grenadines*, Kingstown, St Vincent and the Grenadines.

Thorne, Marjorie (1999) *Report on Women in Politics*, Round Table (October 1998), Caribbean Association of Feminist Research and Action (CAFRA) and the Woman's Forum, Barbados.

Trinidad and Tobago (1995) *National Report on the Status of Women in Trinidad and Tobago:* Prepared for the Fourth World Conference on Women, Beijing, China, September 1995, Women's Affairs Department, Ministry of Community Development, Culture and Women's Affairs, Port-of-Spain.

Trinidad and Tobago (1996) *The Determination and Measurement of Poverty in Trinidad and Tobago: Indications from the 1992 Survey of Living Conditions*, Ministry of Social Development, Port-of-Spain.

United Nations Development Programme (UNDP) (1999) *Report on Stakeholders' Workshop on Women, Gender & Poverty in the Windward Islands*.

—— (2000a) *Sub-Regional Common Assessment of Barbados and the OECS*.

—— (2000b) *Human Development Report 2000*.

United Nations Development Fund for Women (UNIFEM) (1997) *Meeting of Women's NGOs Crisis Centres: Report of Procedings*, UNIFEM, Barbados.

—— (1999) Narrative *Report of a Regional Seminar on Gender and Trade Issues*,

Grenada, UNIFEM, 1999.

Vassell, Linette (1999) 'Gender and Politics in the Commonwealth Caribbean: A Background Paper prepared for the 'Commonwealth Caribbean Regional Symposium on Gender, Politics, Peace, Conflict Resolution and Prevention', unpublished paper.

Williams, Candia (1990) *The Role of Women in Fisheries in Antigua and Barbuda*, Centre for Resource Management, University of the West Indies, Cave Hill, Barbados.

Working Women For Progress (1993) *Report of the First National* Women's *Economic Conference: Women in Search of Alternative Economic Strategies*, Working Women for Progress., Trinidad.

World Bank. (1993) *Caribbean Region Current Economic Situation, Regional Issues and Capital Flows*, World Bank, Washington, DC.

Index

abortion 71

activism 67-8, 71, 74, 77-8, 87, 111-12, 142, 146, 154-6

advocacy 74, 77-8, 84, 90, 95, 112, 134, 137-8

age, care of the elderly 70, 118, 120-1; gender equality 17; population shift 2; programmes for older people 2

agriculture, bananas 6, 100, 117; cash/export crops 5, 7, 9, 26; development projects 29-31; diversification of 7; extension workers in 28-9, 115; food crops 5, 7, 9, 26-8; gender and 27-8, 31, 164; marketing of produce 8, 26-9, 44; monocropping 7-8; national policies 31; pesticides and health 100; plantation system 7; projects 113; sexual division of labour in 27-8; small-scale 7, 10, 26; subsistence 26-8; technology in 28; training in 26-30, 106; women in 8, 25-31, 34, 78, 80, 99-100, 106

aid 5, 144

AIDS 9, 133, 155

Amerindian people 19, 67

Anguilla 1, 130

Antigua and Barbuda 1-3, 8, 18-20, 22, 24, 26-7, 30, 40-1, 48, 62-3, 92, 97, 144

apiculture 46

Asia 32

Association of Caribbean Commissioners of Police 143

Association of Latin American and Caribbean States 4

Bahamas 1-2, 8, 18, 20, 22, 24, 40-1, 64, 94, 130, 140; Crisis Centre 140

banks 10-11, 26

Barbados 1-4, 6, 8-11, 14-15, 18-20, 22-5, 31, 39-42, 49, 51, 61-2, 66-7, 71, 78-80, 82, 92, 97-8, 100, 111, 117, 127-30, 134-6, 138, 140-4, 149, 154-5; Bill on Sexual Harassment 127; BPWC Crisis Centre 140; Bureau of Women's Affairs 66, 128, 142; Democratic Labour Party 61; Department of Gender Affairs 98; Domestic Violence (Protection Orders) Act (1992) 134; Family Services Section (Welfare Department) 136; Men's Education and Support Association (MESA) 154-5; National Organization of Women (NOW) 66, 82, 111, 127; Regional Police Training Centre 144; Regional Tribunal on Violence Against Women 138; Sexual Offences Act (1992) 134; Victim Support Unit 135; Women Against Rape 71; Women's Forum 67

Barbados Workers Union 52

'barrel trade' 43

Basic Needs Trust Fund 126

BELGAR factory 37-8

Belize 1-3, 9, 18-22, 24, 33, 37-42, 62, 64, 67-8, 117, 128, 134, 136-7, 141, 144; Alliance for an Electoral Agenda 65; Belize Organization for Women and Development (BOWAND) 37; Belmopan 38; Civil Society Movement

175

Turks and Caicos Islands 1, 3, 49, 117, 134; Magistrate's Court (Domestic Proceedings) Ordinance (1985) 134

United Kingdom (UK) 2-3, 6
United Nations (UN), Conference on Women (1975) 72, 76, 113; (1995) 85-6, 92, 143; Decade for Women 113; Inter-Agency Campaign on Women's Human Rights 135, 142
United Nations Development Fund for Women (UNIFEM) 6, 85, 138, 142; Campaign on Violence Against Women 138
United Nations Development Programme (UNDP) 67
United States of America (USA) 31, 34
University of Guyana 79, 103
University of the West Indies (UWI) 4, 12-14, 20, 27, 30, 53, 66, 77, 79-81, 87, 99, 103, 150, 153; Centre for Gender and Development Studies 80-1, 85, 87, 103, 150; Child Development Centre 150, 153; Institute of Social and Economic Research 99; Trade Union Institute 53; *see also* CAFRA, WAND

Venezuela 1, 43
Virgin Islands (British) 1-3, 20, 22, 24, 40-1, 62

Windward Islands 1, 6-7, 80, 100, 117
Women and Development Studies Groups (UWI campuses) 77, 79-80; Teaching and Research in Women and Development Studies project 79
Women and Development Unit (WAND) 29-30, 53, 73-80, 87, 112
women, in agriculture 8, 25-31, 34, 78, 80, 99-100, 106; banana collapse and 6, 117; in the civil service 40-1; control over their bodies 71; and development 8, 27, 29-31, 55, 58, 71, 74-7, 80-1, 87, 94, 99-115, 157-68; as household heads 3, 19-21, 109, 118-24, 126, 151;

invisibility of 27, 107; and legislation/legal system 78, 84, 90, 98-9, 134, 137-9, 142, 148; in low-waged labour 8, 15-16, 21-7, 33-40, 71, 77, 118, 122; maternity rights of 34, 56, 99; multiple roles of 30, 105, 107; participation by 30-1, 50-2, 57-69, 100; and patriarchal, male-dominated Caribbean societies 17, 55-6, 58, 112; relationships with men 88-9, 101, 105, 107-8, 114-16, 123-5, 146-56, 157-8, 162; rights of 37-40, 71, 77-9, 84, 86, 90, 98, 142; stereotypical perceptions of Caribbean women 17-19; *see also* gender stereotypes; structural adjustment programmes and 5-6; and tourism 9; trade policies and 6; and unemployment 6, 9, 15, 20-1, 23-5, 33, 100-1, 109, 118-22, 128, 151; and violence 72, 78, 86, 89, 95-6, 98, 108, 114, 117, 119, 123, 125-45, 147-8, 150-1, 154, 156, domestic 78, 98, 108, 114, 117, 119, 123, 127-45, 147-8, 150-1, 156
Women in Development (WID) 55, 71, 74-7, 87, 94, 99, 100, 104-6, 113-16, 157, 161-3
Women in the Caribbean Project (WICP) 99-100
Women's Bureaux/Desks 73, 92-3, 134
Women's Corona Society 70
women's issues 31, 50-1, 53-8, 62-3, 70, 72-97, 104, 111, 127, 159-60, 162
Women's Leadership Institutes 110-11
women's movement 70-92, 112, 147-8, 152, 158, 161-2
women's organizations 70-92, 110, 127-8, 136-9, 141-2, 148, 154, 157, 162, 167
women's professional associations 66, 71
World Bank 2, 5
World Trade Organization (WTO) 7

Young Women's Christian Association (YWCA) 70
youth 25, 34, 46-7, 51, 68, 88-9, 167